a bond servant of the Lord, which we are, but also as sons and daughters positioned in right relationship with our Father. David's passion for the bride making herself ready now is authentic and contagious. Prepare for a shift to take place in your own personal walk as he takes you beyond seeing yourself as just a sinner or servant to also the Bride."

JOE & ANNA BILOTTA
PASTOR AND MARKETPLACE MINISTERS

ENDORSEMENTS

"Wow! I am in awe of David's manuscript. The timing for its release is now. Many of the topics covered—kingdom government, women in ministry, basic biblical functions of the Bride, are sometimes controversial, but mainly ignored by the church at large. The experience I had while reading this work was a greater hunger to see more of the manifestation of the kingdom of God in the earth today. May you experience the same."

REVEREND JOHN PRICE
MOBILIZING APOSTLE

"We have had the honor and privilege of doing life and ministry with David and his family for over thirty years. In that time, we have seen David live the life-transforming revelation contained in the pages of this book. David has courageously presented the truths about present day religion and how we can be delivered into the glorious way God intended us to live. His passion to see the body of Christ living in the fullness of her identity is contagious! He has influenced many with this message and we know that this book will empower you to know your true identity as the Bride of Christ! This book should become a part of every believer's library and referred to often."

SUSAN & JOHN ROVETTO
SENIOR LEADERS, URBAN MISSION, NJ

"David Brudnicki has a strong desire to see the Bride of Christ come alive and *Here Comes the Bride* depicts how Christ wants his church to be. David's desire is for believers to be the most glorious people on planet earth and it's time for the body of Christ to live into this vision. The Church has not fully comprehended her role, and it will require much intention and renewing of our minds and spirits for this reality to take hold. As David says, the Bride of Christ was intended to be the most incredible, attractive, creative, and phenomenal entity on the face of the planet in every age, and it's time that we take hold of this vision. The key to this is developing the relationships we need with God and one another and doing church government His way. This book brings up many good points, and anyone wanting to see an impactful thriving, loving church should give this a good read."

AL & RONNIE IANNUZZI
SENIOR LEADERS, URBAN MISSION, NJ

"If you are searching for a deeper revelation of the Bride of Christ, you will love this read. This book reveals the Father's heart and His relentless desire for us to step into our rightful place as sons and daughters, a place of deep intimacy once lost in the garden and found at the cross. Throughout the ages, settling for knowledge of the Father over an ever-increasing relationship with Him has stunted our growth and delayed our destiny. We were created to be glory-carriers in all the earth and it's time to get ready. *'Here Comes the Bride.'*"

LISA MELILLO
EXECUTIVE COACH, LEADERSHIP CONSULTANT
AND MARKETPLACE MINISTER

"*Here Comes the Bride* was birthed from David's own personal walk and transformation that occurred in his own life. It will challenge and stretch you as he takes you through a fresh look at the church's call to come up higher *NOW*. To see herself as more than just

HERE COMES THE BRIDE

DAVID BRUDNICKI

HERE COMES THE BRIDE
BY DAVID BRUDNICKI

Copyright © 2017 David Brudnicki. All rights reserved. Except for brief quotations for review purposes, no part of this book may be reproduced in any form without prior written permission from the author.

Prepared by:

LIFEWISE BOOKS

PO BOX 1072
Pinehurst, TX 77362
LifeWiseBooks.com

Interior Layout and Design | Yvonne Parks | PearCreative.ca

To Connect with the Author:
www.LeadersServ1st.com

ISBN: 978-0-692-25396-0 (Print)
ISBN: 978-1-947279-15-5 (Ebook)

DEDICATION

To my amazing wife Ruth, and my children Hannah, Jeremy, and Hadassah.

You incredibly bless my life with love, joy, and happiness.

TABLE OF CONTENTS

Acknowledgments	11
Introduction	13
Chapter 1: The Glorious Bride—Where Is She?	15
Chapter 2: Who Are We? How Do We See Ourselves?	29
Chapter 3: Who Does God Say We Are?	41
Chapter 4: Government by the People, for the People	55
Chapter 5: Government by God for His Bride	69
Chapter 6: Alignment and Submission: Enablers or Oppressors?	87
Chapter 7: Is the Marriage Supper Today?	109
Chapter 8: The Bride Made Ready	125
About the Author	143
Works Cited	145

ACKNOWLEDGMENTS

Thank you to those who have gone before me.

Thank you to those who are pursuing God for what He has yet to reveal to humanity.

Thank you to the great men and women of God who have influenced my life and these pages.

I am forever grateful for your devotion to Jesus Christ and His Glorious Bride.

INTRODUCTION

The Christian church as God defines it is intended to be a glorious Bride that is prepared to meet Jesus the Bridegroom, who has given Himself to secure her life and beauty for all eternity. While I believe many in Christianity would agree with this statement, I would argue strongly that most, if not all, believe this is a future event. I have written this book with the belief that the Bride of Christ is arising, realizing that in every generation and season God has called his Bride to be as glorious as she will be on the day that Jesus returns.

For as far back as I can remember, this vision has been in me. For many years it has been clouded and sometimes hidden by my own unbelief, insecurity, and rebellion. Now God has quickened this to my heart, and I embrace fully what I know he has coded in me before I was in my mother's womb. The Bride of Christ is readying herself for marriage. She is coming into her own. She is beginning to understand her identity and the opportunity God has given her. Momentum is building, church government is being restored, and the Bride is maturing and preparing to demonstrate the glory of God as never before seen in the history of humanity. You will hear this declaration over and over throughout the pages of this book. It's intentional. The Church for so long, centuries for that matter, has not fully comprehended her role, and it will require much intention and renewing of our minds and spirits for this reality to take hold. I am thrilled to be a part of His Bride.

CHAPTER 1
THE GLORIOUS BRIDE— WHERE IS SHE?

"Let us rejoice and be glad and give the glory to Him, for the marriage of the Lamb has come and His bride has made herself ready. It was given to her to clothe herself in fine linen, bright and clean; for the fine linen is the righteous acts of the saints. Then he said to me, 'Write, 'Blessed are those who are invited to the marriage supper of the Lamb.'" And he said to me, 'These are true words of God.'" [1]

God's intention in every age, since the offering of His son to humanity, is that those who receive His great invitation would constitute a glorious Bride on the earth in their generation. I have great expectation, hope, and anticipation that the Body of Christ is moving with greater intention and pace than ever before toward becoming His glorious Bride in every generation. Thanks to a great move of apostolic reformation over the last several decades, many great men and women of God are leading the body into a greater manifestation of its destiny than at any other time in history. If we are going to be perfectly honest, outside of the few centuries immediately following Jesus' resurrection, the Church, or Bride of Christ, has been less glorious than God intended except in limited cases and places.

The verse in Revelation reads, "For the marriage of the Lamb has come and the Bride has made herself ready."[2] It is very interesting that as in other places of scripture, here again the words imply action to be taken by the Bride. God's incredible gift of His son to humanity provided all that was necessary for His Bride, the Church, to make herself ready. It will not happen unless the Bride decides to make herself ready. The Body of Christ or Bride of Christ was intended to be the most incredible, attractive, creative, and phenomenal entity on the face of the planet in every age. We have only seen glimpses of this throughout history since Jesus rose from the grave. That is changing rapidly in our day.

In late 2011, God gave me a picture of the Bride of Christ, and it was a timeline, beginning with the resurrection of Jesus. He showed me the centuries that had passed since the resurrection as if they were years. In the first year, the Bride of Christ was a totally dependent infant which relied completely on the Father for its welfare, and as a result of her complete dependency, she was incredibly glorious. Many lives, families, and cities were radically changed in that first century. Since as an infant the Bride only knew the government of Heaven as her strength, she embodied great demonstrations of God's glory on the earth. She impacted cities and nations in ways that have not been seen since. As the Bride grew, each century she became more capable in her own strength and knowledge. As early as age three or four, in the third and fourth century, the Bride became less dependent on Father God and His government, and more independent and organized around religion and politics. As the years and centuries went on, God showed me that the Bride went her own way. She strove for independence and self-reliance. She adapted to the kingdoms and ways of government of the age. She distanced herself from oversight and government, maybe not outwardly, but by her actions.

> *"For an answer Jesus called over a child, whom he stood in the middle of the room, and said, 'I'm telling you, once and for all, that unless you return to square one and start over like children, you're not even going to get a look at the kingdom, let alone get in. Whoever becomes simple and elemental again, like this child, will rank high in God's kingdom. What's more, when you receive the childlike on my account, it's the same as receiving me.'"*[3]

She began to live and act the way earthly kingdoms live and act. She used war and politics to achieve her goals, leaving behind the fullness of His presence that so identified her as God's Bride as an infant. Jesus reminds us in Matthew 18 that we have to become like a little child to enter the kingdom. Amazingly, He does not say you have to become like a little child to have Him, but to enter His kingdom. A lot of Christians believe they have Him, but they do not have or are not living from His kingdom. His Bride, in the vision God showed me, lost her child's heart and the ability to be governed from Heaven. This is evident in our history within the centuries where the Bride lost her way, referred to as the Dark Ages. Where was the Glorious Bride? Where was the light she was intended to shine? She grew into her teen years from the 12th century all the way up to the 20th century and, although with some exceptions such as the Reformation, lived as though there was an arranged wedding coming rather than in intense anticipation of and adoration for her coming Bridegroom.

She spent centuries trying to establish a kingdom without Heaven's government. In much of that time, she used force and ungodly methods to bring about conversion. She moved rapidly away from the freedom she experienced as an infant, where God's presence and the power of His Holy Spirit used her to establish the early church, to an entity governed by control, tradition, and rules. In certain centuries, wherever parts of the Bride realized the need to become a child again and re-covenant with the government of Heaven, they were persecuted, imprisoned, tortured, burned at the stake, and put to death. What had been achieved so vibrantly and brilliantly by the Holy Spirit in her infant years was now a shadow of the past. No longer would healing, miracles, deliverance, and hope be her reputation. It was replaced with formalities, practicalities, intellectual reasoning, and man-inspired rituals. Time after time, remnants of the Bride would arise and realize she had lost her first love, only to be overwhelmed by the forms and dictates of organized religion.

He then showed me the Bride reaching her 20th birthday, or the 21st century, and beginning to awaken to a sense of her real destiny and purpose. She had awakened to the desperate need for mothers and fathers in her life to guide her. She became aware of how her quest for significance outside the boundaries of covenantal relationship with the Bridegroom and her Father, had diminished her glory over the centuries of her development. Her independence and sometimes outright rebellion had caused her to wander through her teen years. She had tried different suitors and advisors over those centuries, all the while desiring the fullness that God had promised, always striving with new programs and techniques but never quite embracing His government as her guide to her glorious maturity.

Then, He showed me His Bride discovering in an even greater sense her passion for the Bridegroom and humanity. God made me understand that in the years since the turn of the 20th century, the Bride has been rapidly accelerating in maturity and getting herself ready to be the glorious mate of the Bridegroom at the marriage supper of the Lamb. He also showed me there has been, and always will be, in every generation the opportunity for the Bride to be the most glorious expression the earth has ever seen. She was always intended to be the most incredible, fantastic, beautiful, creative, and attractive entity in every age. I believe we are in the age where she is maturing into a Bride that has never been seen before. She is coming into her own with great momentum for the coming years. I am so excited!

God's purpose in sending his son Jesus to die for the redemption of humanity was not solely to rescue us as individuals and grant us a life of happily ever after. It is much greater than that. Jesus gave himself for humanity so that we, upon receiving His great gift of redemption, could become the current demonstration of His glory.

Jesus said, "The glory which You have given Me I have given to them, that they may be one, just as We are one; I in them and You in Me, that they may be perfected unity, so that the world may know that You sent Me, and loved them, even as You have loved Me."[4] Jesus gave us His glory, the glory that He had received from the Father. What was His purpose for doing so? So that we could say we have it? So that we could tell people that don't have it they are deficient? He gave us His glory so we could display it the same way He displayed it, so the world would know Him and know the Father through Him. Something has gone wrong along the way. The reason I wrote this book is that I have a heart to see the Body of Christ fully functioning in its destiny as the Glorious Bride. Not at some future time, but now! Today, and every day, just as God intended.

"His Bride has made herself ready." This implies action on the part of the Bride of Christ. Let us remember that the Bride is a collection of every tribe and every tongue, not an individual or collection of individuals. I am more convinced than ever that the lack of a glorious Bride in the earth today is due to the dysfunctional government that the church has been under for many, many centuries. In fact, for some parts of the Body of Christ, it seems like heresy to believe that as a member of the body you have to do anything but accept Jesus as savior. This limited theology of accepting Jesus as my Lord and Savior in itself as the complete work of God has been so engrained in Christianity at large, for so long, that we have large segments of Christianity who do not even know they were called to demonstrate the glory of God, much less believe they could or should.

You are going to hear the terms "Heaven's government" and "Glorious Bride" over and over throughout this book. The reason is we have been so conditioned, governed, and taught the opposite or much less than that for so long, that it is going to require hearing and receiving our inheritance over and over for it to take hold of our hearts.

It's hard to believe that so many Christians worldwide, but especially in America, are having so little impact. It appears the Church believes its finest role is to separate itself from society at large and wait for the return of Jesus. Where we get this notion, I am not sure. It is not in the Bible. Let me be clear here. I understand that the church does good things in a lot of cases, but doing good things and demonstrating the glory of God are two very different things. I also understand that the Bible says in the last days, "Most people's love will grow cold."[5] We have been in the last days since Jesus rose from the grave. When hearts grow cold and sin increases, this is not a time for the Bride of Christ to shrink back, but a time to shine all the more brightly, not with better arguments, judgments, or condemnation, but with the works of Heaven. Jesus fed the poor, but He did so miraculously. Recall the time Jesus was teaching the multitudes and it became late in the day. His followers came to Him and said, "Send them away so they can go and get something to eat." Jesus replied, "They do not need to go away; you give them something to eat!"[6]

His expectation was that His followers were prepared to do the miraculous works of Heaven that He had already commissioned them to do. They were focused on the natural, seeing with their earthly eyes; He was focused on Heaven, seeing with the Father's eyes. It is important to recognize that in this example, His followers did not yet have the indwelling of the Holy Spirit. They had the authority and anointing that He had previously given them to do the works of Heaven, but they did not recognize their authority to apply it to this hungry crowd. Jesus challenged them to feed the crowd. They did not yet have the revelation of who they were. He was stretching them.

When they replied that they did not have any way or capacity to feed the crowd, He asked them, "What do you have?" They brought Him what little they could muster in the natural, and He showed them how the government of Heaven produces more than enough. He set the demon-possessed free with the power of God, not with self-help programs. He healed the sick, raised the dead, etc. all by the power of God and for the glory of God. Now either He is, "The same yesterday, today, and forever," or He is not. We, as His followers, cannot have it both ways.

Jesus gave himself to bring many sons and daughters to glory. Interestingly, if you speak to most believers these days, they do not see themselves as sons or daughters. They may have a notion about being a son or daughter in eternity, but today they believe they are sinners saved by grace. I happen to believe that also. A lot of believers today act like slaves and bondservants even if they would not necessarily refer to themselves that way. Their actions give them away. They do not believe it is the Father's good pleasure to give you the Kingdom.[7] As a result, we have millions of Christians today believing that they are filthy sinners saved by grace for some future day. Jesus said this in Mark 1:15: "The time has come," He said. "The kingdom of God has come near. Repent and believe the good news!"[8]

He also taught His followers to pray in the present: "Your Kingdom come, Your will be done on Earth as it is in Heaven."[9] If it's all about a future adoption and a future Kingdom, then why did He pray, "On Earth as it is in Heaven"?

I myself spent many years in the church hearing alternatively that we are all sons of God and that we were all unworthy, underserving sinners. It was not that my identity in Christ wasn't being preached, it was that the opposite was also being preached. I vacillated constantly between being a loved son and being a stray sheep. I'll admit that most of the issue was probably me; I just couldn't get it. I lived, however, for too many years torn between these two beliefs. Every time I was convinced I was a loved son, I was reminded that pride was the greatest evil. Thinking less of myself was actually championed as true humility. Many times, within the same meeting, I would have an overwhelming sense of hope invade my heart only to be starkly reminded by the end of the teaching how dysfunctional I really was. There seemed to be an unspoken sense of merit in being able to declare who was the worst sinner when we gathered for services.

I am not blaming the leaders that I followed in those times. I know without question that they loved me and wanted the best for me.

In fact, if it had not been for those leaders in my life through those years, I do not believe I would be alive to talk about it. I know they did the best they could through the revelation they had, much of which came from the leaders they were raised under.

As I look back at those times, however, it is my experience that even though the whole gospel was being preached and taught, there was not a full or complete government to support the God-intended growth of sons and daughters of the King into their mature destiny and purpose intended for every believer. It was an environment not unlike many other churches then, and I believe still many today, where it is common to see believers of many years, even decades, who have not made the transition to sons, daughters, and beyond. They still see themselves as more "sinners who have fallen short," rather than "seated in Heavenly places with Christ." Somehow the culture and government produced believers who were saved and even filled with the Holy Spirit, yet living as pre-resurrection sheep. This culture could not mass produce glorious members of the body as God intended. In order to grow into the Glorious Bride, there has to be a culture where everyone is in the growth process. A fully functional government has to be in place to enable God's glorious Bride to completely mature.

Our identity in Christ is co-heirs, co-laborers, a people group raised up to sit in heavenly places. How can filthy sinners sit in heavenly places? The answer is they cannot. What we too often miss is that filthy sinners are who we were. The Bible says that in Christ we are the righteousness of God. "But now apart from the Law the righteousness of God has been manifested, being witnessed by the Law and the Prophets, even the righteousness of God through faith in Jesus Christ for all those who believe; for there is no distinction." [10]

Jesus paid the price for you and me to be glorious representatives of Himself and his kingdom here and now on this earth. Due to resistance to revelation, limited government, and narrow religious teaching, we have been led to believe and live as though we will barely be acceptable to God, and if He is gracious enough, we will make it into His kingdom. This is not God's heart at all, nor was it ever. This is man's interpretation of the lifeless Word, and this results in controlling people and keeping them from being all they were intended to be, whether intentionally done or not.

I believe there is good reason why the church is not nearly as glorious as Jesus died and rose to make her. I believe it is due to dysfunctional government. It is clear to me that Jesus died not only to offer us citizenship in the Kingdom of God, but He also installed the government of God that would produce a glorious Bride in every generation.

> *"For a child will be born to us, a son will be given to us; and the government will rest on His shoulders; and His name will be called Wonderful Counselor, Mighty God, Eternal Father, Prince of Peace. There will be no end to the increase of His government or of peace, On the throne of David and over his kingdom, To establish it and to uphold it with justice and righteousness from then on and forevermore. The zeal of the Lord of hosts will accomplish this."* [11]

Isaiah the prophet told us He would come, He would be our governor, the government would rest on His shoulders, and it would be ever increasing. We have not experienced this except in small ways and small places. Where the government of the King has been received, honored, and practiced, it has produced great glory and continues to do so. However, it also draws the strongest criticism from the larger body of Christianity. Both individually and corporately the church has been mismanaged, and up until the last fifty or so years, has not at all understood or embraced the government Jesus gave us to succeed under.

I hope to take you on a journey of understanding where we currently are and where we are going, depending on how we choose to be governed in the future. I believe it will challenge you to confront what you believe about who you are in Christ and what government you have submitted yourself to. Again, I remind you that Revelations 19: 7-8 says, "The Bride has made herself ready; fine linen, bright and clean, was given her to wear."12 (Fine linen stands for the righteous acts of God's holy people). The Bride John speaks of here is not an individual. She demonstrates the fullest picture of Heaven on Earth when she is aligned with and governed by leaders who serve her from the government of Heaven.

The Glorious Bride can only arise in any generation when the believers take their rightful place as sons and daughters of glory. This can only happen when believers are under a government that produces sons and daughters, mothers and fathers, kings, priests, ambassadors, co-laborers, and co-heirs just as His word proclaims. Jesus gave himself to give us life and a government that enables us to flourish and display the glory He possessed from the Father. The world desperately needs to see the manifestation of the sons and daughters of God in the form of the Glorious Bride today and in every generation. There has been a steady dismissal in western culture of Christianity that has accelerated over the last century. This is happening despite more Christian scholars, more Christian literature, and even the rise of mega churches. This is beginning to change. Many pioneering leaders recognize that the Bride of Christ is still not living out of the fullness of the new covenant government and therefore have re-covenanted with the entire five-fold government of Heaven. These individuals are completely convinced that there is so much more Heaven to be experienced here on Earth than we have encountered.

God is re-awakening his Bride at this time on the earth. It is about government, the government of Heaven. Heaven's government, however, is not the destination, it is the foundation the Bride of Christ arises on. The revelation of how essential the government of Heaven is to the fullness of the Bride's glory is rapidly expanding in the Body of Christ. The Bride is recovering her identity, and she is realizing her need for alignment and submission. She understands that relationship with the King and alignment with His government is the key to her glory on the earth. This is not a denominational happening, and it is not a religious happening. It is the organic, authentic, powerful, magnificent Bride returning to her inheritance and destiny.

This is happening in individuals as they receive the revelation of the importance of Heaven's government in their own hearts, and it is happening in families as God restores marriages and turns the hearts of the fathers back to their children and the hearts of the children back to the fathers. It is happening in the corporate Body of Christ as believers everywhere hunger for more of His presence than ever before. There is a unity spawning in the Bride, which will demonstrate her diversity, her uniqueness, and her royalty to all she interfaces with. The Bride is preparing herself for the best days the earth has ever seen. As her glory increases, it will startle and capture the attention of all the kingdoms and cultures of the world as they observe the Bride of Christ in all her excellence and magnificence. I add my voice to the many who have gone before me and the many who are leading her ascent and say, "Here comes the Bride!"

ENDNOTES

1. Revelation 19:7-9
2. Revelation 19:7
3. Matthew 18:2-5 (MSG)
4. John 17:22-23
5. Matthew 24:12
6. Matthew 14:16
7. Luke 12:32 (KJV)
8. Mark 1:15 (NIV):
9. Matt 6:10, (NIV)
10. Romans 3:21-22
11. Isaiah 9:6-7
12. Revelation 19: 7-8

CHAPTER 2:
WHO ARE WE? HOW DO WE SEE OURSELVES?

"But as many as received Him, to them He gave the right to become children of God, even to those who believe in His name, who were born, not of blood nor of the will of the flesh nor of the will of man, but of God." [1]

Jesus said those who received Him were given the right, power, and authority to be the children of God. It was not out of their own strength or ability, but solely by His sacrifice and belief on the part of those who would receive Him. It is more challenging to me every day to understand how so many people across the globe, but specifically here in the United States, identify as Christians, yet there is so little of the demonstration of the glory that God told us would be characteristic of His followers. Jesus said, *"Whoever believes in me will do the works I have been doing, and they will do even greater things than these."* [2]

These are members of the Glorious Bride who have not been born of flesh and blood only, or by the will of men, but by the glorious grace of God Himself. This is not a future grant of a right that Jesus is speaking about here. It is an instantaneous transformation from the kingdoms of darkness and of this world into the incredible kingdom of light. This is not a deferred right. It is a present inheritance intended to fill planet Earth with sons and daughters of glory! *"Truly, truly, I say to you, he who believes in Me, the works that I do, he will do also; and greater works than these he will do; because I go to the Father."* [3]

Somehow that has been lost, or more accurately, systematically eliminated from the identity of the church. We have to go all the way back to the first few centuries to find church culture really moving in the fullness of the glory for which Jesus died and rose. There have been examples of glorious movements across the centuries since, but they have always been in limited areas and for limited duration. In addition, when these glorious movements have broken out, they are usually criticized, mocked, and judged, not just by the unbelieving world but by the established church. We have settled for a knowledge-based, human system at the expense of the glory that He destined His followers to live in. How did that happen?

It occurred over the centuries of church history, and the primary vehicle for its occurrence has been church government, or lack thereof. Since the early church, our church history has been one of control and knowledge. However, Jesus died and rose to make us free. Religion always enslaves people. Christ sets them free. Jesus said, "You search the scriptures because in them you think you find life, but I am here." He said this to the most religious people of His day. He says the same thing to those bound to religion today!

WHO ARE WE? HOW DO WE SEE OURSELVES?

We have had many generations taught that knowledge was the most important aspect of their walk with God. The inference is that somehow an increase in knowledge equates to maturity and an ever-increasing relationship with Jesus. This has left our relationship with Him defined by what we know and not by *who* we know and *how* we know him. Paul said, "From now on we recognize no one according to the flesh," meaning our understanding is no longer defined by our capacity for knowledge, but by relationship. There will always be more of Him to know. No matter how deep, how intimate, or how intense our relationship is with Him today, there is always much more. This more can only be experienced in relationship. We can study Him, but it is interaction with Him that transforms us from glory to glory, not study alone. *"Therefore, from now on we recognize no one according to the flesh; even though we have known Christ according to the flesh, yet now we know Him in this way no longer."* [5]

We have to ask why has this happened? Was it intentional? Did our forefathers intend for us to be churches and believers that had intellectual knowledge but very little demonstration of glory? I would say it was somewhat intentional, whether consciously or not, and it was also a ploy of the enemy in baiting the church into believing that knowledge would be a good alternative to a glory-bearing relationship. Whenever the glory of God breaks out like it did on the day of Pentecost, it will either continue to grow organically, or it will die from constriction.

More often than not, the stewardship of those leading can allow the freedom of God to propel the people into their glorious destiny. However, those in leadership default to control. Control is the enemy of freedom. Control is the antithesis of service. Jesus said, *"If anyone wants to be first, he shall be the last of all and the servant of all."* [6] Control is also a subtle ploy of the enemy. It is meant to bait leaders into an approach that sees people as sheep in need of management. Yes, there are plenty of scriptures that are used to propagate this glory-less approach. Unfortunately, their use is misguided and does not produce the Glorious Bride that Jesus gave himself for.

The Bible has so much to say about who we are in Christ. Of course, we are saved by grace, but that is our entry point into relationship with Jesus and the start of our maturity as the Glorious Bride. For a part of my life, I did not understand what receiving Jesus as my Savior really meant. I lived with a limited understanding of the King and His kingdom. Part of the reason I lived that way was because that's how I was taught. It was implied that it was more spiritual to act as though I was worthless, but God in His mercy would receive me anyway because of Jesus. Yes, this is true. It was God's mercy towards me in giving me His Son that reconciled me to Him. However, His intention was for me to become a son, a grand demonstration of His glory, not a scarcely saved sinner. I experienced the use of scripture to control, to manage down any thoughts of worth, to make sure I stayed humble. Familiar scriptures such as: *"For it is time for judgment to begin with God's household; and if it begins with us, what will the outcome be for those who do not obey the gospel of God?"* And, *"If it is hard for the righteous to be saved, what will become of the ungodly and the sinner?"* [7]

Time and again, I was reminded that even the righteous would barely make it into the kingdom. I know now that the intention of these reminders was to keep pride in check and somehow facilitate humility. It didn't work. It can't work. God never planned to create a people group who loathed themselves and lived life with a sense of worthlessness. Then there was Isaiah 64. I may have heard these verses spoken on over 300 times over a twenty-year period. *"For all of us have become like one who is unclean, and all our righteous deeds are like a filthy garment; and all of us wither like a leaf, and our iniquities, like the wind, take us away."*[8]

These sermons regularly reminded me that I was barely going to make it even though I was a part of God's household. It may seem insignificant, but scriptures like these reminded me of what I couldn't become. I don't believe it was intentional. This was the identity of the government I was under. The understanding that Jesus died and rose to raise up a glorious Bride was always a distant promise. The present sense was, *"The one that endures to the end, he will be saved."*[9] This was the prevalent culture of my Christian upbringing and so many others that I know. The notion that if we struggle, if we beg, if we don't think more highly of ourselves than we should, if we stop others from thinking more highly of themselves than they should, then we will all squeak into the kingdom of Heaven. The, *"It is easier for a camel to go through the eye of a needle,"*[10] scenario is preached so often in so many places. Instead of an all-out focus on who we could be, who God intended us to be, and how He intended us to be, we settled into what the government of church was ruling with. In some limited, narrow ways it actually sounds noble.

We will live small, restricted, and self-deprecating lives so we can qualify for His kingdom. As large parts of Christianity governed and taught this way, we systematically eliminated the ability to think about the potential for humanity that God had impregnated us with. We became unable to see solutions, healings, miracles, and inventions as ways to demonstrate God's glory. We defaulted to criticizing and judging humanity for its inability to live gloriously, yet we ourselves could not demonstrate the glory they should be attracted to. Denying or living as less than the Glorious Bride of Christ is not humility or an entry ticket to the kingdom of Heaven at all. It is unbelief!

Talk to believers today and ask them how they see themselves. One of the most common responses you will get is, "I'm a sinner saved by grace." Now that is true for all who believe in Jesus as their savior. The problem is this was intended to be the beginning of their faith. If I come into relationship with Jesus on the day He returns, that will be the maximum glory I can display here on earth. If I come into relationship with Him any day prior to the day of His return, then living any day as only a sinner saved by grace is living in a place that denies the glory that He intended us to live in. With all deference to the author, one of the great hymns of the church is called, "Only a Sinner Saved by Grace." If you're over twenty-years-old, it's likely you know this hymn by heart. It truly summarizes the identity crisis the church has suffered over the centuries, and I would like to suggest there is nothing glorious about living as if you are only a sinner saved by grace. The song says, "This is my story, to God be the glory, I'm only a sinner saved by grace."[11]

I am not criticizing this song. I am challenging us to understand songs like this, as well as the government and teachings it grew out of, have conditioned centuries of believers to live on the death side of the cross. What we hear through the ages and still in large part today is that the cross is key. The cross becomes the focus. Now the cross is the key factor in our redemption, but it is a means, not an end. We were never intended to live there nor go back and revisit time and time again. Jesus died once for all who would believe in him, but He passed through death into glory and is seated at the right hand of the Father.

It's fair to say that the overwhelming majority of Christians today live their life at the cross. They have never understood that they died once just like their Savior and that on their day of salvation, they passed just like Jesus from death into life and glory. They live their life believing they don't deserve to be in the kingdom, yet because of His grace they made it. This is partly true, but it's an extremely narrow and damaging view of what Jesus actually gave Himself for. It's quite void of glory. Remember, He gave himself for a glorious Bride! Again, much of church doctrine would condition us to believe that the Glorious Bride is a future Bride. That is NOT the whole truth. We are called to be in every generation the Glorious Bride. Sure, there is the final Bride when He returns, but the belief that it is a future moment as opposed to a now moment has conditioned millions of believers to live a glory-less existence.

The Bible says creation waits in eager expectation for the children of God to be revealed.[12] Talk to any believer today, and most will tell you that scripture speaks of a future occurrence. They either believe it's the day Jesus returns, or they believe in some future generation there will be a move of God that manifests these sons and daughters of glory. It never occurs to them that today is the day, and they are the sons and daughters of glory that God intended to walk the earth and demonstrate His glory in their generation. They cannot think that way because they do not understand who they are. They see themselves as sinners, present tense, saved by grace, filthy rags, and errant sheep. What they don't know is they are sons, daughters, co-heirs, co-laborers, ambassadors, kings and priests, to mention a few things God sees them as. That is His current view of His family not a future view!

Here is another familiar scripture that has defined the culture of the church and the mindset of many.

> *"To some who were confident of their own righteousness and looked down on everyone else, Jesus told this parable: 'Two men went up to the temple to pray, one a Pharisee and*

> *the other a tax collector. The Pharisee stood by himself and prayed: 'God, I thank you that I am not like other people—robbers, evildoers, adulterers—or even like this tax collector. I fast twice a week and give a tenth of all I get.' But the tax collector stood at a distance. He would not even look up to heaven, but beat his breast and said, 'God, have mercy on me, a sinner.' I tell you that this man, rather than the other, went home justified before God. For all those who exalt themselves will be humbled, and those who humble themselves will be exalted."* [13]

Jesus was attempting to draw a contrast to motive and position of heart. It is true that it is His great mercy that has rescued us and brought into right relationship with the Father, and we need to remember how far we were from Him at one time. Unfortunately, the notion that degrading ourselves equates to humility has a very strong foothold in Christianity. Somehow, we are more justified if we act like we are worthless sinners. We have taken a sincere moment in a man's life when he comes to a clear revelation about who he has been and made it a central part of church life. If we think, believe, and declare that we are sinners, we are justified. It is not true. We were sinners. What we forget about this tax collector and so many other examples in the Bible is that Jesus had not yet died, and so this tax collector is responding out of Old Testament culture and not even aware there is the righteousness of God available in Christ Jesus.

Why don't most believers understand who they are in Christ? They have not been raised and governed as sons and daughters. They have submitted themselves to dysfunctional government that has not propelled them into the fullness of their glory but has attempted to control them, leading to lives of diminished glory. In fact, most believers look, behave, and believe more like recovering alcoholics than they do glorious representatives of the living Savior. The major tenet for Alcoholics Anonymous is that you will always be recovering. This is such a strong foundational identity of a prior alcoholic that they actually declare it over themselves repeatedly until it becomes who they are. They will never be free or who they were intended to be because they will always be limited by this identity. I understand it is certainly better to live without an addiction to alcohol than to live with it, so it's great people have changed their behavior through the program.

At the same time, they have to constantly manage the outcome and remind themselves that they are defective as a warning to stay who they have become. Sound like any believers you know? They only know themselves as worthless sinners. They can only reference their lives from that perspective. They even confess over their lives that they are recovering sinners. They may not use those exact words, but listen and you will hear it. They have not moved into freedom as sons and daughters of God but work tirelessly to manage their lives to keep from relapsing. Their mind is so programmed as a recovering sinner they don't believe they can be anything else until they get to Heaven.

Living this way severely diminishes who God is and what He has done through Jesus our Lord and Savior. God didn't send His Son to only die for us, He sent Him to die as us—meaning when He died, He died as you. When you receive Him as your Lord and Savior you are resurrected in His righteousness and glory. We receive adoption into God's family and instantly become co-heirs and inheritors of all He purchased for us in His death and rebirth. Once we come into relationship with Him we are no longer filthy rags, wanderers, or recovering sinners. We are the righteousness of God in Christ

Jesus. Yet we don't see the great majority of believers living this way. We are redeemed to live from glory to glory. Here, now on the earth. We are to be living ever more gloriously from day to day. Yet we spend most of our time managing our behavior and trying to get smarter or learn more about how to stay in recovery. We surround ourselves with other recovering sinners and we worship together, thereby ensuring that the Glorious Bride God intended for this age cannot arise.

Look around. It's pretty clear right now that the church is having a limited impact on society. Many would argue it is the end times, and there will only be a remnant. This is just not scriptural and will not be defensible before the Lord. People are searching for reality. They instinctively know they were created for something bigger. They will not respond to a gospel that does not demonstrate a glory that is the fullness of Christ Himself. They aren't interested in another set of rules. They aren't looking for a twelve-step plan or a set of spiritual laws that will propel them into recovering sinner status. They are seeking something glorious. They are desperate for adoption, acceptance, and validation. They want to believe they are glorious. The only way they will see it is when we live it. When you walk as a glorious son or a glorious daughter, Jesus radiates into their lives through you. Jesus said, *"if I be lifted up from the earth, will draw all men unto me,"* [14] Traditionally, we have been taught to believe He is referencing His death on the cross. That is a very limited interpretation. Jesus is speaking about redemption, not death. His death does not draw us, His life does.

That interpretation is full of death and not life. When He is acknowledged in His right place at the right hand of the Father, when we agree with Him that we are presently seated in heavenly places with him, and when our lives demonstrate His transforming resurrection power, there will be ever increasing levels of glory flowing out of our lives. People are captured by His glory when they see us in this place, not as recovering sinners living by rules and will power, but by His glory that has so altered our lives, so changed our identity, so demonstrated His love they have to respond. They may not always receive Him, but they cannot argue with who we are. We have so allowed His presence to saturate us with His glory that unbelievers can no longer identify with who we were. We are not recovering from anything. We are living gloriously and having a glorious impact on humanity and the planet, just like our Savior did. When He is lifted up in us, He will draw all men unto Him.

I remember a conversation I once had with a believer. He told me if he made it into the Kingdom of Heaven, he would fall face down on the street and just stay there. This believer was a person who had spent over sixty years faithfully serving God. He had been a faithful giver and church member. He had brought up his family in God's ways and was sure to leave behind a legacy of believers for God's future work. Yet at this moment, this believer was saying he was so unsure God would receive him that if he actually made it into His presence, he would be satisfied to just fall face down and stay there. I understand that at some level we all think this way.

However, for this believer, he was making a decided statement about his own worth, or more accurately, the lack of it. What we have to ask is how much of the goodness of God did this believer miss during his lifetime because of this diminished view of self and of God? It is hard to believe we can be saved and part of the Body of Christ, yet be so unaware of all that He has purchased for us to live in now, in this present life. If we hold such a poor understanding of our worth to God here in this life, how can we demonstrate His glory in any great measure? If we are of the mentality that He will barely receive us, how can we live as though He has, "seated us with Him in Heavenly places"?[15] When we choose to believe we have less value than He has declared, we have opened the door to the enemy to hinder our life and our growth. Jesus said, *"God so loved the world that He gave His one and only Son."* [16] He so loved us. He so loves us. When we are in Christ and agree with anything less than He loves us extravagantly, we cannot live in the fullness of His glory, and we cannot represent Him as He intended.

ENDNOTES

1. John 1:12-13
2. John 14:12 (NIV)
3. John 14:12 (NIV)
4. John 5:39
5. 2 Corinthians 5:16
6. Mark 9:35
7. 1 Peter 4:17 (NIV)
8. Isaiah 64:6 (NIV)
9. Matthew 24:13
10. 1Mark 10:25 (NIV)
11. Gray, J.M. "Only a Sinner Saved by Grace." *Hymnary.org*, https://hymnary.org/text/naught have_i_gotten_but_what_i_received. Accessed 4 August 2017.
12. Rom 8:19 (NIV)
13. Luke 18:9-14 (NIV)
14. John 12:23 (KJV)
15. Ephesians 2: 6-7
16. John 3:16

CHAPTER 3

WHO DOES GOD SAY WE ARE?

"But as many as received him, to them gave the power to become the sons of God, even to them that believe on His name." [1]

Let us take a deeper look in scripture and focus on who God says we are. There has been plenty of focus on who we were, but the Bible is full of scriptures about who and what we are in Christ. If you think like I did, you may not think these scriptures are for you or for now. However, they are for you, and they are for now. They are the truth that God has spoken over you, and in order to become a son or a daughter and to truly move into your God-given destiny, they have to be fully appropriated in our lives.

"'And I will be a father to you, and you shall be sons and daughters to Me,' says the Lord Almighty." [2]

"For you are all sons of God through faith in Christ Jesus." [3]

> *"But when the fullness of the time came, God sent forth His Son, born of a woman, born under the Law, so that He might redeem those who were under the Law, that we might receive the adoption as sons. Because you are sons, God has sent forth the Spirit of His Son into our hearts, crying, "Abba! Father!" Therefore, you are no longer a slave, but a son; and if a son, then an heir through God."* [4]

It's odd to me that many people believe we will be sons and daughters when we get to Heaven but do not believe the same at the moment we receive Jesus. This has a dramatic impact on how we live our lives, how we fit in to the Bride of Christ, and how we impact humanity. We are here for one reason, and one reason only. We are here to demonstrate the glory of God so all humanity can have an opportunity to see His splendor, grace, and majesty. This is supposed to be the present reality of the Bride of Christ here on earth. Why is it He says we will be sons, we will receive adoption, and yet many of us live as orphans and foster children?

There is a progression in our natural lives that begins when we are born and continues until we die. It is the progression of growth and learning. We have probably all witnessed or been close to a newborn infant, but I wonder if we ever thought about what that infant thinks or knows. I think it's safe to say in the very first days and months of a newborn's life there is not much thinking or evaluating going on from a mental perspective. The majority of what is taking place is a response to natural senses and physical stimuli. A newborn who is hungry reacts and cries out for food. We would all agree a newborn has no sense of who they are. While it is true they are in fact someone's son or daughter, it's not something they can comprehend because they have not developed the capacity to think and understand yet. There is a point in the future when each newborn will develop a greater understanding of who they are and what the concept of family and relationship means, but as a newborn they just react out of need.

There are great parallels in our spiritual life. There is to be a progression, an ongoing maturing. This process is intended to take us from slaves and orphans to sons and daughters, from sons and daughters to mothers and fathers, and from mothers and fathers to kings, priests, ambassadors, co-laborers, and co-heirs. Much of Christianity is focused on salvation. I do understand the importance of that. However, seeing people born again and not growing into all God intended them to be is not what God planned or designed. We would never be okay with that in the natural. Why would we think God is OK with it in our spiritual development?

God promised us that through the gift of His son all who would believe in Him would become a part of His family. The scriptures say Jesus is the first born of many sons and daughters. He came in the fullness of time not just to rescue us and secure a future promise, but to renew us and join us to the family of God and the kingdom of Heaven for the present and for eternity. He gave us His Holy Spirit as the seal of our adoption for the here and now, not for a future time. When we get to Heaven, we will not need a seal of adoption; we will be a family with all those who have been adopted in to the kingdom. The seal of the Holy Spirit is for our walk here on Earth in this life. He has been given to us so we can live life in an ever more glorious way—a way that demonstrates Christ in us, the hope of glory.

> *"See how great a love the Father has bestowed on us, that we would be called children of God; and such we are. For this reason, the world does not know us, because it did not know Him. Beloved, now we are children of God, and it has not appeared as yet what we will be. We know that when*

> *He appears, we will be like Him, because we will see Him just as He is. And everyone who has this hope fixed on Him purifies himself, just as He is pure."* [5]

Over and again, the Word of God tells us who we are in Christ Jesus. Here in John's letter we are again told how the great love of the Father has enabled us to become sons and daughters through the extravagant offering of His Son. It seems that we have received the letter of this promise, but not the spirit of it. In my experience, many in the Body of Christ have received and lived the "called the children of God" part of this scripture but have missed or not grown into the "and such we are" part. There is a world of difference in what we call ourselves and what we really are.

When we call ourselves children of God and then live like orphans, the world questions our confessions. The kingdoms of this world are orphanages that want to destroy relationship and family. A Christian should be a brilliant alternative. When we live as children of God, the world doesn't know us because we are living far more gloriously then we were once capable of living. They knew us before we became children of the King, and the fascinating change that occurs in a real son and a real daughter is something the world sees and says, "That is not the person I once knew."

Throughout the word of God there is always a "now" and "then." Yes, there is a "then," but when we defer everything to "then" at the expense of now, we are not at all living as the children God intended to carry His glory to the nations. John states emphatically, *"Beloved, now we are the children of God."* [6] Yes, you, me, and all those who have received Christ as their Savior are instantly children of the King.

Think about the newborn child again. When the child is born, we don't say to ourselves, "because it is not clear what they will become, they are not a son or a daughter." That would be absurd. The moment they are born, even at the moment of conception, they are sons and daughters. It will take time and work for maturity to occur, but that does not change their status in the family.

When we get to the, "we will be like Him," of course there will be transformation. We will be moving from a fallen, broken world to a place where evil and brokenness no longer exist. Our mandate, however, is to live in the fullness of His family as sons and daughters until that time. It is to purify our hearts to such a degree that the fullness of His glory and presence saturates the people and places He has put us on the earth to present Him to.

We are taught and conditioned to believe that His glory is only a "then" thing. The Word of God repeatedly states that it is a "now" thing. We are so convinced that the world is going to hell in a handbasket that we excuse ourselves from having any responsibility for changing it. Too many who call themselves children of God have not had the "now" revelation. They continue to live powerless to their surroundings, and as no threat to the kingdoms of this world because they have not fully appropriated the fullness of their adoption into the kingdom of His great Son. It is the Spirit of God that seals our adoption.

The process of adoption as it relates to a child in the natural is such that on the day of adoption there is little notion of family, of belonging, or of the reality of the great miracle that has just occurred from the adopted child's perspective—especially if the child is a little older and has some understanding of what is happening. The child is cautious, apprehensive, and concerned about the future. It will take time, nurture, intense love, and care for the child to feel sealed into his or her new family.

> *"For all who are being led by the Spirit of God, these are sons of God. For you have not received a spirit of slavery leading to fear again, but you have received a spirit of adoption as sons by which we cry out, 'Abba! Father!' The Spirit Himself testifies with our spirit that we are children of God, and if children, heirs also, heirs of God and fellow heirs with Christ, if indeed we suffer with Him so that we may also be glorified with Him."* [7]

The Apostle Paul writes, "All who are being led by the Spirit of God are the sons of God." Notice the terminology. He does not say "led" but "being led," meaning it is a continuous process of constant growth into maturity as sons and daughters of God. It is the Spirit of God who sealed our adoption and who leads us into ever-greater glory, guiding us from slavery, fear, and apprehension into our position in God's family, where we then exclaim with absolute confidence, "Abba, Father." What a progression! In Christ, we are moved from a spirit of slavery into a spirit of adoption where we understand our identity in Christ. It is Holy Spirit who continues to witness to our hearts about our identity as we yield to him. He also continues to nurture and mature us into heirs of God, fellow heirs with Christ. I believe historically we have viewed this promise in the context of the last part of the verse, meaning that most view the promise of sonship and inheritance as contingent upon our suffering with Him so that we may be glorified with Him. I am not saying we will not suffer with Him or for Him. What I am saying is that all of this - the adoption, the growth, the inheritance, and yes, even the suffering, is a now promise and not a future promise. It is not that we *will be* sons and heirs, suffer and be glorified. It is that we *are* sons and heirs, and we suffer and glorify Him now. He is already glorified. It is God's intention that we be glorified to demonstrate Him.

The Body of Christ should be the most effective, interesting, exciting, and attractive entity on earth. I believe that is happening now, and it will accelerate as we receive greater revelation of who we are. It will happen when the body at large begins to live as generations of sons and daughters, fathers and mothers, secure in their adoption, walking in the fullness of all Jesus walked in. It is not that way today, at least not for the majority of Christianity. We do not have many fathers and mothers living out of the fullness of their identity because they were not raised as sons and daughters in the fullness of the spirit of adoption. They were raised as straying sheep who would be scarcely saved. When you are raised this way, it is impossible to reproduce sons and daughters in any greater level of family than what you yourself were raised in, unless there is a radical shift.

It is of utmost importance that we make the transformation to sons and daughters. If we cannot or do not make that transition, it is unlikely we will grow into healthy fathers and mothers. Healthy fathers and mothers mature into kings, priests, ambassadors, etc. When I say healthy, I mean the maturation process is not a competition, but it happens in an honoring, humble way. Maturity happens by progression. It is not always tied to natural age. It can occur as rapidly as we allow the truth of what God has secured for us in the offering of his Son to become the truth that rules our lives. The church was intended to be full of sons, daughters, fathers, mothers, kings, priests, ambassadors, etc. In this ecosystem in which everyone is doing their part, sons and daughter honor fathers and mothers, and each honors the other through the process of maturing into greater glory, then the glory God intended accelerates.

> *"I'm not writing all this as a neighborhood scold just to make you feel rotten. I'm writing as a father to you, my children. I love you and want you to grow up well, not spoiled. There are a lot of people around who can't wait to tell you what you've done wrong, but there aren't many fathers willing to take the time and effort to help you grow up. It was as Jesus helped me proclaim God's Message to you that I became your father. I'm not, you know, asking you to do anything I'm not already doing myself."* [8]

The Apostle Paul speaking to the Corinthians explains to them that though they may have many teachers, they will not have many fathers. He himself had become a father to those God had given Him authority over. I love the way *The Message* translates it. As a father, Paul wants to help his sons and daughters to grow up well, not by harping on what is wrong, but by appropriating and investing in what is right. He also wasn't interested in having sons and daughters for His own sake. We see from his interaction with his spiritual son Timothy that Paul was propelling him into all that had been spoken over Timothy's life. Paul wanted Timothy to mature into the fullness of glory and destiny God had intended for him. Paul wasn't looking for more followers of himself. He went all over the territory raising up leaders for the growth and service of the body. The promises of God in Christ Jesus are that as we walk in greater intimacy with him, He will father and mother us into glorious maturity. Paul could speak this way because he had traveled this road himself. He had passed from being a slave to religion to being a son of God. He had allowed himself to be fathered by other believers and now was himself fathering sons, daughters, kings, priests, and ambassadors. Just think about how many leaders were nurtured and matured by Paul's faithfulness and willingness to serve.

"Guide older women into lives of reverence so they end up as neither gossips nor drunks, but models of goodness. By looking at them, the younger women will know how to love their husbands and children, be virtuous and pure, keep a good house, be good wives. We don't want anyone looking down on God's Message because of their behavior. Also, guide the young men to live disciplined lives." [9]

While there are not many references to strong women in the New Testament, there are enough. Some of this has to do with the predominantly male culture of the times. Yet even in a culture where women had little value, we have testimony of some incredible women. We see Mary as the mother of Jesus, carrying both the purpose of raising Him and the sorrow of knowing His earthly mission. Mary endures the scorn of her community and the shame heaped upon her for being pregnant out of wedlock. It is a challenge to find a male in the New Testament who endured as much as Mary did to birth and steward God's plan of salvation in her day.

Then there is Elizabeth, who is faithful for many years even though she could not have a child. She perseveres in her faith and believes in the goodness of God until she sees it realized. She, like Mary, lived through the rumors and the gossip. She endured who knows how many teachings that barrenness was a curse from God. Yet the Bible says that she was faithful in all things.

Then there are the women at the tomb. They are all there before the men. They are the first to see the empty tomb and the first to see Jesus after the resurrection. There is Anna the prophetess, who prophesies over Jesus at His birth. There are amazing women all over the New Testament, and even though the Bible does not detail many of their lives, it is very easy to believe that all these women and others played a very prominent part in mothering the early Church into its maturity.

The Body of Christ desperately needs fathers and mothers to raise its sons and daughters into maturity. This is something that is missing or not clearly understood in the body. This is costing the church the proper growth and nurture of its children into glorious adults who are prepared to raise future sons and daughters of God into fullness. When we think about ministry, we often think about familiar roles such as teachers, evangelists, and pastors, and while they are necessary, they are not the only leadership roles necessary for the Glorious Bride to be revealed.

Too often, the roles of mothers and fathers in the body do not get the recognition or the value they deserve in the healthy eco-system of developing maturity in the Body of Christ. Many times, those who have traditional leadership roles have not themselves transitioned into healthy mothers and fathers. While they are ministering from their calling, many do not or cannot see themselves as sons or daughters, much less fathers or mothers. When we have a leadership role and we do not have a reasonable sense of our own identity and place in the family, we tend to re-create in our own image. We end up raising children who are no more mature and glorious than we are.

The importance of the process of growth and maturity cannot be understated. Too often in the church, only a handful of people have made the transition to full maturity. These are the ones who understand who they are in Christ. They have made the transition from slaves and dependents to sons and daughters, fathers and mothers, kings, priests, and beyond. Part of the process of becoming sons and daughters requires understanding that we need mothers and fathers to facilitate our growth. We willingly submit to mothers and fathers because we know their hearts are to propel us into the limitless future God has purposed us for.

Submission to authority is a real challenge in the church these days. Much of that stems from improper fathering and mothering. The predominant model of spiritual parenting today is to father and mother through rules and control. As we ourselves become healthy mothers and fathers, we achieve a level of maturity that prepares us for greater responsibility in the kingdom. We learn that control and tradition will never achieve what love and relationship were intended to birth. We mature to understand the roles of king, priest, ambassador, co-heir, and co-laborer as a great honor and a great necessity for the glory of God to be revealed through His body. As fathers and mothers, we anticipate and rejoice when we are used to propel sons and daughters to places that are beyond what we might have reached ourselves.

> *"...until we all attain to the unity of the faith, and of the knowledge of the Son of God, to a mature man(woman), to the measure of the stature which belongs to the fullness of Christ. As a result, we are no longer to be children, tossed here and there by waves and carried about by every wind of doctrine, by the trickery of men, by craftiness in deceitful scheming; but speaking the truth in love, we are to grow up in all aspects into Him who is the head, even Christ, from whom the whole body, being fitted and held together by what every joint supplies, according to the proper working of each individual part, causes the growth of the body for the building up of itself in love."* [10]

There is greater glory to be revealed. The Apostle Paul clearly defines the process of growth and maturity. He tells us that we are not to remain children. Children, more often than not, do not think of others and do not understand responsibility or have the capacity to do so. They think narrowly and selfishly. They struggle with authority. This is a process. It takes family and authority to properly nurture God's children from orphans into members of the Glorious Bride of Christ. Entrance into the kingdom of light is the beginning, not the end. Greater glory is always God's intention. For the Bride of Christ to enter into her most glorious moment in history, it will take sons, daughters, fathers, mothers, kings, and priests all working together. Now these roles are not fixed in time or title. Depending on our level of maturity and who it is we are interacting with, we can function in any one of these roles.

Take a great leader in the Body of Christ. Even great leaders need mentors and advisors in their lives. What's the point? The point is there is never a time when we do not need to be aware that all these roles are necessary for a healthy Christian and a healthy Bride. A great leader needs to be a son or a daughter so he or she can receive inspiration and encouragement from others, and so it is with each role. We need them all to achieve the fullness God so intended for His Bride. The body, His Bride, is to be a company of lovers, believers who have understood their inheritance and agree and align with the government of Heaven. This government builds people up. It is intentional; it gets underneath people and raises them up so they can rise higher and burn brighter. It creates an environment where maturity is demonstrated and expected, a system where all know their place and promote the growth and maturity of all others.

This only happens in a sustained and healthy way when we have His government. It's not man's government, or even church government, but the government that Jesus died to install. Isaiah prophesied that the government would be on Jesus' shoulders and the increase of

His government would have no end. It is His government, properly installed and administered, that facilitates souls becoming sons and daughters and maturing into mothers and fathers, kings, priests, and ambassadors. Without His government, it is impossible for the Bride to achieve the glory He intended. For many centuries, we have not fully embraced the government of Heaven. We have not lived from who God said we are. We have not released all that Jesus died to secure for us. It is as though we have decided to live on kingdom food stamps rather than access the freedom, potential, and glory that God has always planned for His Bride. The promises of God are plain and real. They are for now and for the future. It is time to take Him at His word and see them fulfilled.

ENDNOTES

1. John 1:12 (KJV)
2. 2 Corinthians 6:18
3. Galatians 3:26
4. Galatians 4:4-17
5. 1 John 3:1-3
6. 1 John 3:2
7. Romans 8:14-17
8. 1 Corinthians 4:14-16 (MSG)
9. Titus 2:1-6 (MSG)
10. Ephesians 4:13-20

CHAPTER 4

GOVERNMENT BY THE PEOPLE, FOR THE PEOPLE

"For a child will be born to us, a son will be given to us; And the government will rest on His shoulders; And His name will be called Wonderful Counselor, Mighty God, Eternal Father, Prince of Peace. There will be no end to the increase of His government or of peace, on the throne of David and over his kingdom, to establish it and to uphold it with justice and righteousness from then on and forevermore. The zeal of the Lord of hosts will accomplish this." [1]

We are having a great awakening in the Body of Christ with regard to our glorious identity. Many are teaching on the revelation of who we really are in Christ. However, knowing who we are but not knowing what governs us will prevent the Bride from the fullness of her glory. Understanding our identity and our inheritance in and of itself will not enable the fullness of the Bride to come forth. It takes Heaven's government—not the government we are used to in our everyday lives, but superior government: the government of Heaven.

Isaiah declares Jesus as our governor of an ever-expanding government, a government in which there will be no end or limit to peace, justice, and righteousness. When we look at life here on earth, we find that success is usually a result of gifts, effort, and talents governed well. It is the same for the Bride of Christ. For her glory to be revealed in the spectacular way God intended, her gifts, talents, and efforts will need the ever-increasing government of Heaven to enable her. Let's think about some simple everyday life examples. We have made Christianity and the kingdom of Heaven very complex, and it was never meant to be that way. God intended the offer of redemption and eternal life to be simple and available to every human who has ever walked the plant. This is practically demonstrated when the Bride of Christ is fully functioning in the kingdom government of God.

If we look at the process of human birth, it would be very difficult to imagine that the child to be born could reach the fullness of its potential without a set of principles to guide the child's life. Without people, especially mothers and fathers, it's highly improbable the child will be nurtured and propelled into his or her destiny. There is evidence today showing good government is key for development and the birth process, even before birth, right from the moment of conception. Think about how many children are born on the planet today with no significant sense of government coming from their parent or parents. Again, there is data showing children born in challenging circumstances have a much higher set of risk factors than those born where care and government are prioritized.[2] If a mother and father were to participate in the conception of the child and then expected it to take care of itself upon birth, we would all agree these parents should be charged with negligence.

The child is helpless. It needs guidance, food, safety, affection, relationship, and much more. It needs a governmental structure to thrive under. The child needs someone to think about what is coming, someone who clearly sees the future and is making preparations to propel the child forward. The child needs someone to feed it, to care for its daily needs, and to manage its safety. It needs someone to teach it so it can learn the functions and behaviors necessary to living a successful life. Someone has to be there in the child's life to call out the greatness, to see the giftings and talents, and to exhort and encourage the child into them. Someone needs to bring the child into a relationship with its creator, introducing and demonstrating Jesus to the child so the child can know its greatest hope is Jesus himself. This is why the word of God places such an emphasis on children as being an inheritance from God. Parents, optimally fathers and mothers who are in right relationship with God themselves, provide the most effective governance for children that can be administered on the earth. It is true not every child has the blessing of both parents, but that is where the Body of Christ fills the void. All of these functions and more comprise the government that is necessary to ensure a newborn has the greatest possible chance for healthy growth and success.

As the child grows, its needs will change. A structure has to be in place that assesses those changes in needs and adapts accordingly. Boundaries have to be set and reset as the child progresses from one stage of growth to another. The child has to be given freedom to experiment and to take risks so that he or she develops the proper skills necessary to manage the challenges of life at the next stage of development. The child needs to learn to handle failure and how to adapt and be resilient. It would be hard to argue that a young child is aware of these needs. Competent parents providing good government ensure that the child is protected and safe as he or she navigates all these necessary elements of the maturation process.

Think of the family. We have talked about the individual, but the same concepts for the individual apply when we think about family. We have stretched the very definition of family in recent times, and it is very alarming that a high percentage of children being born today are born to single parents. This puts the family government at risk from the very beginning. Even with these challenging definitions of family, it would be hard to argue that a family can be successful without some level of functional government. We need someone thinking about the support and needs of the family. The future has to be considered, at least to some degree. Relationships, safety, growth, education, and health all need attention if the family is to exist, function, and potentially thrive.

Each family member has differing needs, talents, and passions. It is up to the parents to govern each member in a way that propels them into their passion or destiny. What works with one will not work with another. It takes a discerning, fully-functional government to enable an environment in which each member can excel. Some will mature faster, some will fail more, some will be like mom or dad, some will not. It is critical that the family government acknowledge each member and nurture each in a healthful way. It is also crucial that parents not demand their children be vehicles they can live out their dreams through. It is the parent's role to serve the children so they can excel and be all God intended they be, not what the parents decide or desire they be. The parents must govern with a generational mindset, meaning they are not just governing for the now. They are governing with a vision for their future generations. Exodus 20:5-6 says that He holds parents accountable for their sins for four generations, but He shows His love to those who keep His commands or govern well to a thousand generations. Imagine if the Body of Christ had a revelation of how important government is, so much so that they lived with a thousand-generation outlook!

Now let's think about the work place. If you have ever been employed, you will encounter government in the work place. Employees do not just show up to a location every day and do want they want, when they want. No business would ever survive under such a government. Whether it is a small private business, a large corporation, or the public service sector, employees come under a set of concepts and principles that define how the business operates, what is required to make the business successful, and what their role is in that environment. In fact, for midsize to large corporations, there are entire departments that manage and set corporate governance. Just being an employee does not equate to success in business.

In the last three or four decades, many great leaders and books have addressed the issue of governance in the corporate world. Many times, these have been focused on one person, typically a CEO who has been very successful in some industry, who attempts to impart the formulas for success through a book. In reality, however, it is never about one person, no matter how smart they are. Even when one person has a great idea or a great invention, it takes a significant amount of people and resources to see that idea or invention come to life, and that process requires a fully functional government. We have great publications coming out of some of the country's top business schools addressing the concepts and theories of corporate governance and leadership. In the corporate environment, we have departments called human resources, operations, research & development, sales, and corporate strategy. These departments comprise the government of the business. Without this government, the business could not survive, and it certainly could not thrive. If you read business books these days, you will hear terms like visionary, networker, manager, organizer, entrepreneur or achiever, activator, empathizer, futurist, or strategist. These are all related to governing styles.

There is much excitement in the business world for developing good government, identifying the people with governing capacity, and ensuring they are in the right role. All this effort is with the intention of making the business better and driving success. This is the heart of good business government. The goal is to set up the offices and policies that will give the business the best chance to reach its potential. Typically, businesses that do not take into account all these functions of government do not reach their potential. Think about a business that only performed sales. It might do well for a short time, but when the product exceeds its life cycle or competitors develop a better model, the business will fail if it has only focused on one product. Good government enables us to look beyond where we are. It looks at the future, it fuels creativity, and it cares for the health of the current environment so that it becomes the soil of new ideas and new inventions.

Businesses are spending tens of millions of dollars annually to create successful corporate culture, otherwise understood as government. In a good culture, businesses help employees understand the vision, the mission, and the corporate objectives, as well as foster communications, resilience, and working across boundaries. We all know of great companies where the culture is highly valued. The last 20 plus years has seen a great emphasis on diversity. It is now understood that diversity brings together the best possible mix of talents, backgrounds, experience, and knowledge. It allows businesses to more accurately represent the customers they serve, and it gives the business keen insight into different customer needs they could not previously discern.

Think about the many facets of operating a business and the skills and knowledge required for each function. Think further about how much effort must go into making sure each function is aware that all the other functions are equally important for the finished product or service to be successful. Much effort goes into corporate governance to ensure that individual function or department goals are complimentary and support the overall goal of the business.

Think about the functions of corporate strategy, research and development, operations, sales, and marketing. Imagine a business where there was not a high value on respect and communication between these key functions. It would result in a highly dysfunctional business. It is important to note here that this business is not dysfunctional because it doesn't possess the skills, talents, and giftings necessary for success; it is dysfunctional because of its inability to govern those skills, talents, and giftings in a way that enables the best possible outcome. The willing and valued cooperation and interaction of the key functions of corporate governance is what allows some companies to far out-perform their competitors.

Additionally, over the last few decades, there has been a significant movement away from top down governance in business organizations to a more bottom up approach. It is commonly referred to as a horizontal governmental structure, or a flatter structure. All employees in the company have talent, ideas, innovation, and creativity in them. The movement is towards ensuring that everyone is engaged, heard, and seen. This is critical to the success of the business, and most successful corporations of the last few decades have fully embraced it.

While these highly successful companies have visionary leaders, they also recognize that it takes every single employee at every level of the organization for the company to be successful. The companies that are leading performance in their business sectors today are the ones who have embraced a more relational, empowering structure for their organizations, as opposed to the positional top-down structures of the past. The structures of the past typically achieved success in the short term but were not all able to sustain it due to the inability to keep employees engaged and believing they were part of something great. This shift in governance empowers employees to take risks, make decisions, and even fail because often it is in the failures that great lessons, the next inventions, products or services are discovered.

Now, let's look at government from a different angle. Let's look at people who leave their country to move to another country. More often than not, people choose to do this to find a better life than the one they are experiencing. Since I am an American, I will use my country as an example. Currently, America is having plenty of discussion about immigration and how to properly address the challenge it presents us as a country. The question to ask is, why are people coming here in the first place? I believe the answer, without a doubt, is government. People come here because the government allows them the best possible chance to be successful and pursue their dreams. Interestingly enough though just arriving on the soil of America does absolutely nothing to make you successful. What your arrival does do is put you under a government whose principles and functions create an environment where you can choose to be successful.

When you align with the government, and respect and honor all its functions, then you put yourself in the best possible position to thrive under that government. You may not necessarily interact with all parts of the government at all times, but you instinctively know you need all functions to be operating optimally for you to have the best chance at achieving your dreams. We probably do not even give it a second thought, but we would never be okay with the department of defense ceasing to function. We take for granted that issues like security, borders, and safety are being cared for. In that environment, we can focus our energy on achieving our dream. We teach our children about the value of government, about its function, and the necessity of each branch. It is inside the structure of the government where each citizen can develop his or her gift, talent, and ability to become what their heart desires. Whether it be in business, service, or any other sector, it is a functional government that enables each person to achieve what they pursue.

Most recently, we have had serious challenges in our government here in the United States. Government has become more dysfunctional than ever due to the breakdown of the honor and respect for all functions and offices. Because concern has shifted from the welfare of all to special interests, party affiliations, and party popularity, our government is more challenged than ever to accomplish things such as passing a budget. Fortunately, for the time being, there is still enough structure and goodwill in place for most Americans to continue to pursue their dreams. However, if there isn't a course correction and renewed vision for our government as a whole, it certainly raises questions about the future. Continued unemployment, waste, infighting, and ignorance of the will of the American people will only delay the country in getting back on track to being the great nation it has been and a great blessing to the rest of the world.

Why all this focus on government? Because without government, everything breaks down, and nothing can be as successful as it should be. What does that have to do with the Bride of Christ? She can never be as glorious as God intended unless she is governed from heaven to earth, not from Earth to Heaven. Unfortunately for the church, we have not embraced Heaven's government since the first few centuries. The church has primarily been governed from

Earth to Heaven, employing earthly principles mixed with talents, gifts, and abilities and some of what God is doing, expecting the advancement and the expansion of the kingdom. That approach, a top-down, positional governmental effort, has led to some success across the centuries, but not anywhere near the glory that Jesus died for the Bride to have.

What we find in more recent centuries, and especially the last one, is the kingdoms and governments of this world have a better understanding of functional government than the Body of Christ does. The body on a whole is more dysfunctional and divided in its government than any entity on the planet. How ironic is it that the very form of government that Jesus gave us—apostles, prophets, pastors, teachers, and evangelists—is being employed on a grand scale by businesses and governments all over the planet while the church remains splintered? It doesn't really matter that the systems of this world don't acknowledge God when they employ the functions of His government. They are blessed because the government of Heaven always produces ever-increasing results.

From the individual to the family, from a team to a business, from a citizen to a nation, those that are successful are those with a fully functional government. For the Bride to arise to her intended glory, the government of Heaven will have to be embraced in every individual heart, every family, and every part of the Body of Christ. Gifts, talents, and ability abound in the Body of Christ today as they have in every age. Rarely, though, have we seen them governed in a way that produces the Glorious Bride.

The church through the ages has unintentionally become like the Israelites in the time of King Saul. The people were restless. They had forgotten how extravagantly God had treated them. They began to look around and see how the kingdoms of man operated. They became envious and desired to be like those around them rather than be governed directly by God himself. They went to God and asked for a king like all other kingdoms. God told them their request would cost them. It was not that He was abandoning them, but they would not have the direct governance of God himself.

As a people, they would lose that reputation of superior government. There are many parallels today. The Church finds itself impotent to affect many situations facing humanity today. Instead of re-embracing the government of Heaven and bringing the King and His government to the issues, the Church has chosen to be like other kingdoms. God has provided His Son to enable all who would believe Him to be a part of His great kingdom. He has given us His Spirit to confirm our adoption as sons and daughters, and He has given us His government to enable His sons and daughters to mature into the Glorious Bride.

We have partly lost sight of this. God's Spirit and His government were to enable a company of believers on the earth to live in a spectacular way, elevating Jesus Christ, the Savior and governor of His eternal kingdom of light. We were intended to be a company of people who not only live God's laws, but exceed them. Jesus said, *"Do not think that I came to abolish the Law or the Prophets; I did not come to abolish but to fulfill."*[3] His Bride was not intended to walk the earth struggling to achieve the law, but to live in such a glorious fashion that she exceeds the law. So when the law says, "Do not steal," those living in the fullness of Heaven's government not only do not think about stealing, they think and behave exactly the opposite, meaning they live to bless and release provision wherever they go and to whomever they meet. They don't just fulfill the law; they far exceed it.

When the law says, "Do not commit adultery," the Bride doesn't just avoid adultery. The Bride so honors and invests in covenant marriage that kingdom relationships display a glory as far from adultery as the east is from the west. She can do so when she has been governed from Heaven by the King's ever-expanding government. Looking at it a different way, whenever His Bride lives below the law and outside the boundaries of the government of Heaven, we steal from humanity the experience of seeing the great glory of God.

All successful government down through history found its roots in the foundational government that Jesus purchased for us. Whether in the church or outside it, wherever we see the foundational principles of Heaven's government applied, we will see a successful outcome. We are on the crest of a great reformation of church government. It has already begun, thanks to many fathers and mothers who have given their lives to the vision of seeing the Bride in all her splendor. It is flourishing in places around the globe. It is about to expand in grand fashion. It requires some radical changes in who we believe God is, what Jesus gave himself to accomplish, and how the Bride sees her mission here on the earth. In a world with growing knowledge and continuously evolving technology, the kingdoms of this world grow ever darker and more desperate. The Bride of Christ is the answer. Her destiny is to be the spectacular demonstration of glory that God promised the earth.

ENDNOTES

1. Isaiah 9:6-7
2. Cabrera et al., "Influence of Mother, Father, and Child Risk on Parenting and Children's Cognitive and Social Behaviors." *Child Development,* vol. 82, no. 6, 2011, https://www.ncbi.nlm.nih.gov/pubmed/22026516. Accessed 4 August 2017.
3. Matthew 5:17

CHAPTER 5
GOVERNMENT BY GOD FOR HIS BRIDE

"And He gave some as apostles, and some as prophets, and some as evangelists, and some as pastors and teachers, for the equipping of the saints for the work of service, to the building up of the Body of Christ; until we all attain to the unity of the faith, and of the knowledge of the Son of God, to a mature man, to the measure of the stature which belongs to the fullness of Christ.

As a result, we are no longer to be children, tossed here and there by waves and carried about by every wind of doctrine, by the trickery of men, by craftiness in deceitful scheming; but speaking the truth in love, we are to grow up in all aspects into Him who is the head, even Christ, from whom the whole body, being fitted and held together by what every joint supplies, according to the proper working of each individual part, causes the growth of the body for the building up of itself in love." [1]

What is the environment, culture, or government that allows entrance into the kingdom and the advance of Heaven here on earth? One that takes orphans and enables them to become sons and daughters, mothers, fathers, kings, priests, and ambassadors. What is the government that will enable the full beauty and glory of the Bride of Christ in every generation? Let us look at the above scripture to see the fullness of what Christ died for. He died not just to save and reunite us with the Father, but to enable our entry or adoption into the family of God and the kingdom of Heaven. No kingdom exists or continues without a government. In Isaiah 9:7, the prophet writes that the government of Jesus will be ever increasing. *"There will be no end to the increase of His government or of peace, on the throne of David and over his kingdom, to establish it and to uphold it with justice and righteousness from then on and forevermore. The zeal of the Lord of hosts will accomplish this."*[2]

It is only under the full government that Jesus himself installed that we can really see the Glorious Bride in her fullness. What we have experienced during much of the history of the church is partial, limited, or dysfunctional government. This is not a judgment or a criticism, it is just the reality. For most of Christianity, except for the very first century church, we have witnessed the church being governed by parts of the government Jesus installed, but rarely by all of it.

The most typical forms of government in the church throughout the centuries has been pastor, teacher, and evangelist. I am not speaking of individuals here, but of the form of government. I believe that when we have the full proper government of Heaven in place, God raises up the right people to lead in the office. It is critical that we have the full government in place. We may not always have a person with that gifting, but we must have the government. When we do embrace the full government Jesus leads, we can trust God to develop the people to take their places. Too many times we ignore significant parts of kingdom government because a strong leader with a specific gifting leads from that strength and does not honor and seek to develop all offices of government.

What is the government that Jesus died and resurrected to install? As stated in Ephesians 4:11-16, it is apostolic, prophetic, pastoral, teaching, and evangelistic. In the last few decades, this has become commonly referred to as the fivefold ministry or government. I have come to really dislike that term. In my opinion, it is thrown around as a buzzword, but rarely do we see this form of government rightly installed and operating. What is more often seen is the church adopting a form of government that fits the gifting and skills of the leader at that time. It is understandable that we work with what we have, but so much is lost when we focus on a person and accept a limited government due to that person's particular strengths. The church then neglects to install the full government of Heaven and does not honor all offices of the government, regardless of whether a person with that specific skill has risen up.

One way I look at the government of the church is like a river. I have never heard of or seen a more glorious description of a river then the one found in Revelation 22:1-5:

> *"Then he showed me a river of the water of life, clear as crystal, coming from the throne of God and of the Lamb, in the middle of its street. On either side of the river was the tree of life, bearing twelve kinds of fruit, yielding its fruit every month; and the leaves of the tree were for the healing of the nations."* [3]

The river of life described in Revelation has to be the most spectacular. It is in this picture I see the full government of God in operation and ever-increasing, just as Isaiah said it would be. I see the bed of the river, its route from the throne of God to its destination as the apostolic office. I see the water that fills the bed as the prophetic office. It is the water filling and following the route that propels the body along its destination in every age and generation. Then we have the life in the river - the fish, plants, insects, etc. These forms of nourishment represent the pastoral and teacher forms of government. Finally, we have the entire river, all the functions of the government working together, enabling the evangelistic function of the government to thrive.

Who can read the description of the river in the verses above and not want to see it, swim in it, and receive its nourishment? When the full government of God is embraced and each function and office is fully honored and working together, it produces glory. It enables the Bride to live so gloriously that she can't help but attract the desperate, the broken, and those separated from the love of the Father. I believe it is most important to get the government back to its original purpose, having the full government of Heaven functioning continuously. It is only in this environment that the Bride in our day can be as glorious as God intended her to be.

John writes in his gospel about rivers of living water flowing out of our bellies. Not just a river, but rivers. *"He who believes in Me, as the Scripture said, 'From his innermost being will flow rivers of living water.'"*[4]

He writes, *"He who believes in me."* This is not just a confession, but an embracing of the King and His kingdom. Jesus said, *"You are my disciples if you do what I say. If you continue in My word, then you are truly disciples of Mine,"*[5] meaning if you live under His ever-increasing government. Think about it. Not only does God's word say a river will flow out of us, He says rivers. What a picture—many rivers all carrying the full force or glory of the complete government of the King and His kingdom. How impactful would that be if we all lived in a way where many rivers flowed out of us, each carrying the fullness of Heaven to the earth around us? It is challenging at times to see one river flowing, much less many. Part of the reason is the river is a symphony of the government of Heaven. Many of us have not understood the government, therefore our flow is limited or distorted.

Let's look hard at the idea of the river representing the government of Heaven. If the route represents the apostolic, and I do not have the water which represents the prophetic, then I have a dry river bed. I still have an origin and may still have a destination, but there is no flow to propel me on toward the destination. I am missing the Heaven to Earth mandate. Without the water, there is no environment for life to spring forth, so the pastoral and teaching offices of government promote a social and intellectual way. There is no supernatural manifestation of the power of God, just logical reasoning and social care. This also severely hampers the evangelism office and often results in using fear and manipulation to attempt to draw people into the kingdom.

We could have the water, the prophetic office, and not the route, the apostolic office. What happens then is there is no sense of greater purpose or glorious destiny. The voice of God and declaration of His intent is manifest, but not a clear direction for what the kingdom of Heaven is to accomplish. Since there is water, I have the environment for producing life and so the pastoral, teaching, and evangelism offices can grow, but there is no long-term sustainability of vision for the kingdom here on earth. Since the foundation of apostolic government has been ignored, the river can flow, but with no route it becomes powerless and winds up self-focused and without impact.

Why focus on these two offices of government? These are the two offices that have been denied, ignored, or just given cursory treatment over the past centuries. The church at large has been a three-office governed body for a very long time, and until fairly recently, has not even acknowledged the offices of apostle and prophet. I want to remind you I am not talking about individuals, I am talking about offices of the government that Jesus installed. Even today, there is much tension in Christianity at large about the role or offices of apostle and prophet. Large segments of Christianity do not even embrace these offices today. They are looked upon as functions that ceased when the last of the original apostles died, or at some other arbitrary time in history. They are misunderstood offices that are more generally rejected then embraced. They have been ignored for so long that Christians at large do not even expect that these functions are critical to their government. Yet the Word of God says they are. *"So then you are no longer strangers and aliens, but you are fellow citizens with the saints, and are of God's household, having been built on the foundation of the apostles and prophets, Christ Jesus Himself being the corner stone."*[6]

The offices of the apostle and prophet form the foundation of church government. All of the other offices are to be built on and propelled by the offices of the apostle and prophet. The forms of government typical in church history have largely ignored these foundational parts of the government and embraced the forms that men have been more comfortable with. It has been easier to embrace a government that we can control intellectually and organizationally rather than the full government Jesus installed. The full government is much more challenging. It requires reliance on God and intimacy with Father,

Son, and Holy Spirit. It is a government intended to serve as opposed to a government that demands service.

When we look at church government centered on the offices of pastor, teacher and evangelist, we see government built on knowledge, performance, tradition, and rules. Now all of these things are also required in the full government model, but without the apostolic and prophetic foundation, these incomplete governments typically fuel organizations much like any other we see on the earth. They may perform good works of service and community acts, but in general there are non-church organizations that do the same things. When we see government solely focused on evangelism, we see many people coming into the kingdom, but they come in as orphans and remain that way because we lack all the other offices that are necessary to propel believers into the fullness of their destiny. The point is, when we exclude the apostolic and prophetic offices, we almost always exclude the supernatural power that God promised would mark those who followed Jesus. *"These signs will accompany those who have believed: in My name, they will cast out demons, they will speak with new tongues; they will pick up serpents, and if they drink any deadly poison, it will not hurt them; they will lay hands on the sick, and they will recover."*[7]

Jesus said His followers would do these things. We would free those demonically oppressed, we would heal the sick, and we would have supernatural protection. Why has this not been the consistent resume of the church? The answer is we cannot have an outcome when we have not fully embraced the government that produces the outcome. Some will say they believe in Jesus and He is everything. Absolutely true; however, when we fully embrace and believe in Jesus, we fully embrace His government. You cannot have a King and not have His kingdom. It doesn't work, nor is it scriptural. Alternately you cannot have a kingdom without a king. You can try, but you will not have the fullness of either the King or His kingdom.

What we have typically witnessed in Church history is more attention has been paid to an individual leader than to the structure or the government. If the individual is a good pastor, then the model of leadership is pastoral and the forward momentum in that environment is to reproduce after kind, so we reproduce pastors. The same is true for teachers and evangelists.

However, if the apostolic and the prophetic centers around a specific individual, it almost always breeds dysfunction. God never intended His government or its offices to be person-centered, unless the person is Jesus Christ. It is true that He does call persons to serve in the government. God calls people to serve His government. He did not create and establish His government to serve the person called.

Think about the state of the current U.S. government. For many decades, it has appeared to be increasingly dysfunctional. There is an overwhelming inability to get anything done or to take on the hard problems of our day and make the necessary changes. There is serious division and polarization. Think now about how the U.S. government came to be. Some person did not stand up and say, "I'm the president," or "I'm the senator." A group of men from all walks of life got together to form a more perfect form of government. This effort was born from great sacrifice, and the government was born—government by the people and for the people. Once the form of government was established, people were called to run for office.

Why is the kingdom government so important? The key lies in Ephesians 4:12-16. Ephesians 4:11 gives us kingdom government offices. It is upon this government we bring Heaven to earth, as well as equip and enable the saints for the great works of service God has prepared beforehand. We hear many teachings about works of service and much effort goes on in Christianity to bring positive change to the earth. However, the fullness of what God declared would occur through His body cannot be realized without the full functioning of His government. When we govern by the King's government, we equip saints rather than controlling sheep. Kingdom government propels sinners to sainthood, creating an environment where growth is encouraged, even required, and ability, talent, and creativity are celebrated. His government creates a culture where the growth from slave and sinner to king, priest, and ambassador happens naturally, constantly, and quickly.

In this government and culture, we do not define people by where they came from; we propel them into where God is sending them. We do not hold people back because they may possess greater talent or gifting; we rejoice when they can exceed what we have been able to achieve because we know that is how the kingdom advances and expands. Maturity is celebrated because everyone in this environment understands that everyone in the kingdom is intended to be absolutely glorious. It is understood we cannot achieve the greater glory intended for the Bride of Christ if we do not value each other and the government. His government is the structure that enables equipped saints to come together in such a profound way: *"...the whole body, being fitted and held together by what every joint supplies, according to the proper working of each individual part, causes the growth of the body for the building up of itself in love."*[8]

Each function of the King's government and each saint under that government comes together in a way that can only happen when all the government is honored and embraced as necessary for fulfilling God's plan for each generation. Each part, office, and person comes together with a synergy that propels the growth of the body, the Bride, in glory and love.

Again, I want to stress that the Body of Christ, His Bride, is called to be the most incredible, phenomenal, creative entity on the planet in every generation. If we are honest, we can admit that she has not been this in any great way over the centuries outside the very first century. Unless we have the foundational kingdom government, we cannot see this fullness arise. We see many church efforts with social, economic and judicial focus occurring in the earth today, and much of it is well-intentioned and necessary. However, it is not having the impact that the Bride of Christ was intended to have. I believe this is because the foundational government underlying many of these efforts is not in place. Efforts built and launched on a limited government cannot allow the brilliance and impact of the Bride to manifest.

The challenge we face starts with church leadership but also applies to the saints as well. Church leaders have to come into agreement with the king's government and become its proponents. They have to recognize that the only way to see the fullness of what Jesus intended for the earth is to embrace the King and His kingdom, the governor and His government. In doing so, the shift in the Body of Christ will accelerate. The body will become an entity led by those called to propel the saints beyond where they themselves have previously attained.

When this occurs, the Bride of Christ will shift from a legacy-based entity that celebrates the great people and things that God did in the past to an entity that sees the glorious future of God's plan, with solutions to every problem on the planet. She will mature into an entity that honors past accomplishment, knowing that we refuse to live in the past. She will know we stand on the great things that God has done in history with the full confidence that, by the King and His kingdom, we live in the acceleration of all that Jesus declared would be characteristic of His Glorious Bride!

When we have church leadership fully embracing and aligning with the King's government, we have the environment necessary for the maturity and advancement of the saints. I cannot tell you how many times I have talked to other leaders and listened as they wondered why more people weren't engaged in the advancement of the kingdom. The reality is many saints are not committed and fully invested because they have not embraced the full government of the kingdom, nor have they been consistently taught to live from the place of kingdom government.

The key to enabling the saints, to unlocking the tsunami of Heaven on earth, is enabling all believers to live under a government that propels them into the fullness of the glory of God. This is to happen now, not in the future. The coming together of the saints, fit together in such a glorious way as to demonstrate the intense glory of Jesus, is the outcome that occurs when the full government of Jesus is installed. Government is essential to prosperity, safety, and peace, to name a few outcomes of good government. Kingdom government was intended to enable a culture where believers are part of a thriving, growing, powerful kingdom that brings Heaven to earth.

My own experience has been an interesting journey. I grew up in a loving, Jesus-focused church environment. While it was common to hear teaching about the government of the kingdom, it was not something that was intentionally pursued. In this environment, there were few folks maturing rapidly or being propelled into the works that God had intended for them. Most of the believers surrounding me were focused on their own shortcomings, their failures, and lack of ability. There was no great momentum to what they did possess, nor a great level of encouragement for where God intended them to go. It was not a culture of vanquishing the impossible from a governmental perspective. This is extremely important. We did have a belief individually and were taught that all things can be accomplished through and by Jesus Christ. We did not, however, have an environment governmentally that enabled the momentum of that belief for all members.

In my own life, I went through some difficult periods—times full of rebellion and unbelief, characterized by my inability to realize that God loved me and created me with a glorious plan in mind. I was always reminded of my faults by others who were more spiritual, more knowledgeable, and who had made fewer mistakes. Attending church functions was at the same time uplifting and depressing.

There were a few people that believed in me so much more than I believed in myself. Nick was such a person. Nick was a hardworking immigrant who could barely speak English but had a heart of gold. He was a simple man who had a profound impact on my life. Every time I interacted with Nick, he had a word of encouragement for me; he would seek me out at meetings to bless me and find out how I was doing. He would discern when I was disconnected from the presence of God and challenge me to go forward. He was consistent, simple, loving, and incredibly necessary to my ability to find my identity. Even when he knew I was off track, he never focused on my failure, but always on my future.

I share this with you because while Nick was not the only one, he was in the minority. Most believers do not understand their role because they have not been taught and do not understand kingdom government. I submit to you that every believer should be a Nick. Anytime we come into contact with a believer, there should be an exchange of glory. The interaction itself should propel all of us into a greater maturity and advancement of the kingdom. The church should not be a culture where there are a few Nicks; it should be an entity where everyone is fully engaged in their destiny and propelling others into their glorious destiny. Interestingly enough, we find this model more at work in the culture outside of the church than inside. When we look at great sports teams, organizations, and institutions, what we typically find is an environment where everyone is completely invested in accomplishing the vision. Everyone understands that to realize the vision, every person involved is valuable.

What do these teams, organizations, and institutions have in common? The answer is they have an enabling government. In fact, I would argue they all have an underlying foundational government that is apostolic, prophetic, pastoral, teaching, and evangelistic. They obviously do not recognize their government that way. They call it strategic, marketing, human resources, research and development, networking, management, and many other terms that are just different labels for the kingdom model. The Body of Christ has the greatest King with the greatest government. We have a far superior leader and government. No team, company, or institution should ever outshine the fullness of the Bride of Christ on the earth.

It is imperative that the Body of Christ embrace, install, and expand the government of His Kingdom. This is not just about the church, but we cannot have the impact we all know we are meant to have on the kingdoms of this world until we embrace and align with the kingdom of our God. Let's take a look at an example of the King's government in place back in the Old Testament. The testimony is recorded starting in 2 Kings 6:8. Here is what is happening: the king of Aram is attacking the nation of Israel. A prophet in Israel, Elisha, is hearing all the king of Aram's plans from God and warning the king of Israel, Joram, about where and when the attacks are going to take place. At this particular time in Israel's history, there is alignment between the prophetic office and the apostolic office. The foundation of God's government is in place and aligned. For this period of time, there is honor and respect between the king and the prophet that allows the plan of the enemy to be exposed and nullified. Remember, this is not happening in the synagogue but in the nation. This alignment impacts the entire nation.

The alignment of Elisha and Joram causes such frustration for their enemies that the king of Aram decides to find out how his plans for Israel's destruction keep failing. He discovers that Elisha is aligned with Joram, and this alignment is preventing his destruction of Israel. The king of Aram sends his army to attack and kill the prophet Elisha. When the army arrives and surrounds Dothan, God moves in a miraculous way. Elisha prays that the army will be blinded, and they all are. The entire army is led into the city of Samaria. Elisha prays again for their eyes to be opened, and they are. They find themselves surrounded by the Israelite army: *"Then the king of Israel when he saw them, said to Elisha, 'My father, shall I kill them? Shall I kill them?'"*[9]

When the apostolic and the prophetic are aligned, there is intimacy and relationship. There is no attempt to demonstrate whose office is greater, whose gifting is more important, or who hears from God more. There is a nation to save. Elisha replies, *"You must not kill them. Do you slay those whom you have taken captive with your sword or bow? Serve them a meal. Let them eat and drink, and then go back to their master."*[10]

Wow! Not the decision we would all make. Interestingly, it is when the foundation of the government is in place, both apostolic and prophetic, that the opportunity arises to negate the enemy's plan and gain access to those influenced by the enemy, not for their destruction but for their nurture. It is due to the relationship between the apostolic and the prophetic that Israel now has a captive audience. The prophet tells the king to feed them. This is so unlike what we think. Many times we think we are here for the destruction of our enemies, and that is true, except our enemies are not flesh and blood. They are principalities and powers. The reason we often miss who our enemies are is because we have not grown up in the fully functional government that Jesus gave us. Anytime we have less than all the government of Heaven guiding us, it will eventually lead to limited glory at best and harming people at worst.

Picture this scene in Samaria. The Israelites have captured the army of Aram. They line them up. The Aram army has to be totally convinced that they will be imprisoned, forced into slavery, or executed. I think it's safe to say that every one of the Aram army soldiers is convinced that life as they knew it is over. They are all told to stand at attention as they watch the Israelites count them. The suspense has to been intense. The leader of the Israelite army assumes position at the front of this captured army as the captives await to hear their final fate. Surprisingly, the Aram army finds itself being invited to a meal by the Israeli army. I am certain that all of the Aram soldiers were thinking this was a trick. As they are led into this great banquet, they desperately try to figure out what is happening to them. They wonder, "Is it possible that we are really going to be wined and dined by the very people we were trying to destroy?" As they sit down, it becomes apparent to each of them that exactly what they were told is happening. They are being served a banquet by the very army and nation they viewed as enemies. They whisper to each other in disbelief. As the reality of what is happening sets in, they turn their attention to their captors. I imagine they begin to ask their captor, "Why are you showing us kindness? Why are you feeding us? Is this some sick torture that you impose on your enemies? Before you destroy them, you throw them a great banquet?"

I picture the Israelites responding and telling the enemy soldiers that this is not a trick; we are going to feed you and return you to your homeland. The Aram soldiers are in complete shock. Why would you let us go? Why would you be kind to us when we were set on your destruction?

The Israelites begin to talk about their God and His goodness. They begin to tell the Aram soldiers that they never really had a chance at all. God had been giving them the Aram army's battle plans from the very beginning. The Aram soldiers are a captive audience. They are now hearing about the incredible works of God. They are being pastored, taught, and evangelized, all because the foundations of the government aligned and submitted to each other, allowing for an incredible sequence of miracles by God to bring these soldiers to the dinner table in Samaria.

Think about it. I am completely convinced some of the Aram soldiers became believers in Almighty God that day. I am further convinced many of those soldiers, upon hearing of the great works God had done in Israel and with His people, said to the Israelites, "I have great needs also; can your God help me? Could your God heal my child, my family member?" I know for sure that every one of the Aram soldiers returned back to their country in amazement at what had just happened to them. Never before had they had a military experience where they had attacked a nation, were captured, and had a celebration thrown for them. When the government of the kingdom is in place, His glory can impact the earth in ways that we see as uncommon and bizarre, but He sees as the natural result of Heaven invading earth.

What we find most of the time in recent centuries is that we have some form of pastoral, teaching, and evangelistic government as the predominant government in the Body of Christ. A closer look at our present circumstances in western Christianity shows this limited form of government is not producing life and healing for the nations. It is generally producing sheep that are co-dependent followers, having limited impact on the world around them and living far less gloriously then God intended. His intention is that His river brings life and healing to the nations. It is time the full government of the King and His kingdom is embraced and restored. It is time for a reformation of church government as God intended it to be and Jesus died and rose to install.

ENDNOTES

1. Ephesians 4:11-16
2. Isaiah 9:7
3. Revelation 22: 1-5
4. John 7:38
5. John 8:31
6. Eph. 2:19-20
7. Mark 16:17-18
8. Ephesians 4:16
9. 2 Kings 6:21
10. 2 Kings 6:21

CHAPTER 6
ALIGNMENT AND SUBMISSION: ENABLERS OR OPPRESSORS?

> *"And Jesus came up and spoke to them, saying, 'All authority has been given to Me in heaven and on earth. Go therefore and make disciples of all the nations, baptizing them in the name of the Father and the Son and the Holy Spirit, teaching them to observe all that I commanded you; and lo, I am with you always, even to the end of the age.'"* [1]

Jesus declared to His followers that all authority had been given to Him and in that authority, His followers should be should be doing all the things they witnessed Him do. As we have discussed in depth in the previous chapter, we cannot assume this command can be accomplished without the government necessary to see it fulfilled. Authority is only meaningful in the context of a government. Jesus is the head of the government both in Heaven and here on earth. Revelation 11:15 reads, *"Then the seventh angel sounded; and there were loud voices in heaven, saying, 'The kingdom of the world has become the kingdom of our Lord and of His Christ; and He will reign forever and ever.'"* [2]

The kingdom of this world is to become the kingdom of Jesus Christ. We tend to push that declaration into the future because we have not learned it is already in progress. The kingdom of the world is becoming the kingdom of our Lord. It is not just a "then" statement. It is an alpha and omega statement, meaning before mankind began and until Jesus returns, the kingdom of this world is becoming the kingdom of Jesus. Furthermore, in His kingdom, where His government is ever-increasing, He shall reign forever and ever. Does that mean we will need the apostolic, prophetic, pastoral, teaching, and evangelistic roles in Heaven? I cannot say. I can say that we need them here on Earth because that is the structure Jesus empowered to transform the kingdom of this world to the kingdom of our Lord.

Many in the Body of Christ are embracing this structure, and I am excited about the prospects for the future Bride of Christ based on that momentum. However, I think we have to not only acknowledge the full government of Jesus, but also test whether we have embraced and enabled its fullness in our lives. When we have completely understood the necessity and purpose of His entire government, we then have to enable it. This is incredibly challenging due to the influence of past church government and the influence of non-church government, meaning the kingdom of this world.

When we look at the state of Christianity today, it would be hard to argue that the church at large is governed as it should be. What we commonly see in church government today are boards of elected officials like corporate boards, with CEO's and directors aligned in a corporate structure rather than apostles, prophets, pastors, teachers, and evangelists aligned in a relational family structure. The church today is by and large an organization run by positional authority. The Body of Christ was never intended to operate in positional authority. Jesus is a relational savior. The Father, Son, and Holy Spirit exist and govern in perfect relationship. Truly, we need structure, but structure enabled by alignment and submission to Him, His government, and to each other. Relational authority enables service driven by love and passion as opposed to performance and fear.

Why is positional authority more common in the church than relational authority? There are a number of reasons. The most important is that over the centuries, the church has adapted to the government culture of the state, as opposed to living out the government culture that Jesus came to bring to earth. We have adopted a kingdom of this world government at the expense of the kingdom of Heaven government.

Why is this a problem? Haven't many organizations thrived employing the corporate governance structure of the culture? It is a problem for the Body of Christ because Jesus asked us to be in the world, but not of the world. His government is other-worldly. In other words, His government was intended to produce such a glorious outcome that there would, and should be, no comparable entity to it on the face of the planet. His government is to bring solutions, inventions, creativity, wellness, wholeness, and all other kinds of blessing to the earth.

The lack of the full embrace of His government over time has caused us to live and exist more like corporations do than like the most compelling, unique group of people on the planet. Corporations exist for one thing: to make a profit. Their leaders are focused around one thing, guiding and governing their business to ever-increasing levels of success, success being defined by increasing profit. The members of the corporation follow leadership because they, too, want something. They want to benefit from the profit the corporation generates. The general understanding is, the better the corporation does, the better its members can do.

The church of Jesus Christ was never meant to be governed this way. The Bride of Christ is a company, which God intended to serve mankind, to miraculously impact humanity with the full demonstration of the glory of God. Too often, we look like a company who is just pursuing more of what God and people can give, and in that governance, we are raising members who are motivated by what they can get, as opposed to what they can give. Since we have adopted the governance methods of the culture, we behave and operate just like the culture. The dominant method of government in the corporate world is positional authority, meaning all levels of authority are structured by position. Rarely does relationship having anything to do with authority. Although there are exceptions, the general rule is that your position in the corporation grants your authority. In this structure, people do what they are told to do because they understand the position holds the authority to determine their future.

The church is a relational entity with a relational government. It starts with God the Father, God the Son, and God the Holy Spirit existing in perfect relationship. It extended to us when Jesus gave himself to restore us to perfect relationship with Father, Son, and Holy Spirit. He did so by coming in the form of man, dying, and rising again, bringing the government of Heaven to earth. He is the ultimate leader, and He alone has ultimate authority over all things. His government is ever increasing. His kingdom is not about expansion for expansion's sake. His heart is relational. His goal is not increase for the sake of Himself. His goal is to carry out His father's wish to have the biggest most glorious family ever assembled for all eternity. Jesus said in John 3:16-18:

> *"For God so loved the world, that He gave His only begotten Son, that whoever believes in Him shall not perish, but have eternal life. For God did not send the Son into the world to judge the world, but that the world might be saved through Him. He who believes in Him is not judged; he who does not believe has been judged already, because he has not believed in the name of the only begotten Son of God."* [3]

God's heart is for relationship. Jesus was sent to secure the opportunity for that personal relationship to be restored. God did not demand relationship but offered it through the sacrifice of His son so we could be made right through Jesus and restored to the Father. God has a position. He is God. He does not govern by His position but by relationship. The church in general is governed by position more than it is by relationship. I believe we think we are a highly relational entity, but the reality is division, lack of honor for authority, and problems in submission give us away. Many times, a church culture seems more like a corporate office than the Bride of Christ. Who is performing to get ahead? Who is making someone else look bad so they can look good? Who is desperately hurting on the inside, but for fear of being rejected, cannot come to the family and get the necessary help?

When we adopt governance in the church that is not the government Jesus decreed, we create a culture where our leaders and members behave and mature in that government. When that government is like the culture, we wind up with all the challenges the culture has. People exist and act on what's in it for them. Both leaders and members operate primarily out of self-interest even when their best intentions are otherwise. They belong to the church, but since they have joined a government which has not fully embraced the government of Heaven, they can only be as glorious as the government they have joined. A lot of church leaders complain members are not engaged, they are not getting it, and they aren't maturing. What they do not realize is their members can only be as glorious as the government they are led by.

When we settle for less than all the government of Heaven, we enable a culture that invites separation and dishonor. In order to fully embrace the government Jesus gave us, we have to repent for division and rebellion. This is strong language for believers. I am not saying we willingly divide and rebel. I am saying since we have not been governed with the full government of Heaven, we have learned to act, think, and respond more like the members of a corporation or an earthly kingdom than like the Bride of Christ.

Alignment and submission have become inflammatory words in church culture in recent decades. They have been given a meaning that implies weakness or loss of self. The reason this is so is due to the prevailing limited government the church has accepted. Remember, Jesus installed the government, apostolic, prophetic, pastoral, teaching, and evangelistic for the propelling of the saints into the good works God had prepared for humanity. When we do not accept and employ this full government, then we mutate alignment and submission into something other than God intended. Leadership in the Body of Christ at whatever level we view it, individually, family, or house church, was intended to be governed fully by a culture that demonstrates alignment and submission so the saints could see the government they placed themselves under was there to nurture them into greater glory. Since the view is limited due to the limited form of government, we expect saints to behave in ways and demonstrate glory that they have not seen or been taught.

If we could accept right now that Heaven's government is what God intended and agree it has to be adopted, we would instantly see the greater glory it was intended to produce. The challenge is we have a learned culture in the church that resists alignment and submission to authority. It is the minority of the Body of Christ today that truly governs relationally, although this is changing rapidly. The majority of the body is governed positionally. The leaders have a title, and churchgoers respond to the power invested in their title. To some degree in the church, this has been extremely exaggerated.

We have set up leaders and allowed them to rule with no accountability. We have elevated talent and gifting over character and service and allowed leaders to be unaccountable for their actions. When we enable positional authority and accept less than the full government God requires, we have a culture that mimics the earthly kingdoms, not the Heavenly kingdom. This hurts both leaders and members of the body. When the goal is to get to the top position because that is where the power is, then relationship is secondary. Performance becomes the road to advancement and drives staying at the top. When leaders find themselves in this position, they most often become a victim of the system. They cannot admit mistakes because it implies weakness and may result in punishment. They retreat from authentic relationship, knowing it will expose whatever it is they are struggling with. Issues needing to be addressed go unchecked. More times than not, these situations result in the leader committing some grievous offense and damaging the Body of Christ. Positional authority in a partial government results in dysfunction every time.

When we accept His government, we also have to reform our understanding and behavior around alignment and submission. Think about the many millions of people who declare themselves to be Christians. Then think about how that many people are not having much, if any, impact on the culture at large, or even their own sphere of influence. Why is that the case? Is that God's plan? It does not appear in scripture. Many Christians are behaving exactly the way they have been governed. That is not to say they have been governed incorrectly, but to say they have been governed incompletely. When we have not been governed in the way Jesus intended, we act, think, and reproduce after the non-church culture, the kingdoms of this world. Our church government looks just like the non-church model.

Think about some of the greatest challenges the church faces in this regard. Let's look at one - divorce. Now if there is ever a time the Body of Christ should be a loud, screaming, glorious demonstration that leads and drives world culture, marriage should be it. Yet in the church among Christians, some data suggests that divorce is just as common as it is among non-Christians. How is that possible? Should not Christian marriage be the hallmark for demonstrating the coming Bride of Christ and her groom Jesus the Savior? Why is the divorce rate an issue in Christianity? There are many reasons, I am sure. I believe one key reason is we have lost reverence and respect for alignment and submission. We have adopted pieces of the government we like and applied them to suit ourselves. We have learned to live in ways that are not consistent with the kingdom of Heaven.

When we disagree, we break covenant and violate alignment. When we want our own way, we refuse to submit. We do these things in our personal lives and our marriages because we think we have a right to. We learned how to behave this way in the church. We have watched covenant breaking and church splits along with violations of alignment. The inability and/or unwillingness to submit has plagued many a church body. Caution is required here. It is not that these behaviors were or are being overtly taught by the church. It is because the church has not employed the full government of Heaven. She has opened the door for the government of Earth to invade the church, and the outcome is the church looks more like an earthly entity than the Glorious Bride of Christ.

What would it look like if the Church had a divorce rate of 0%, meaning that 100% of Christian marriages were flourishing, glorious relationships? Is there any chance we would have to go out and defend the institution of marriage if the state of marriage in Christianity were that glorious? Could anyone argue that it wouldn't cause an incredible phenomenon on the earth if Christian marriages had that level of success? I am not talking about a forced or rigged outcome here. I am talking men and women relationally aligned, submitted to God and each other, not because they have to or because the rules say they should, but because they so understand and align with the government of Heaven they willingly, with great joy, apply it to their lives and relationships. Think about the evangelistic power that the Body of Christ would have right this moment if the marriage success rate in the body was that high. People would be knocking down the doors of churches to figure out how and why.

Think about the impact to society and our culture. We wouldn't need marriage defense amendments and voter referendums on marriage between a man and a woman. The outcome of glorious marriages all over Christianity would be a far greater demonstration of the kingdom of Heaven here on Earth than any law, bill, or vote could accomplish. It would end the debate and echo the Bible in saying the "Kingdom is closer than you think." There would be such an incredible demonstration of alignment and submission coming together in glorious covenant. Men and women would be in relational harmony, just like Jesus and His Bride. Think about the impact on our children and future generations. Every child born from these incredible relationships would have the benefit of seeing what marriage should look like. They would grow up under a relationship that has Jesus as it's King and His government as it's foundation. Our children would not be drawn to the kingdom of this world for relationships because the glory would be so great among Christian marriages, it would be near impossible to want anything but that kind of blessing for your future.

Many would argue that is an unreasonable outcome. One-hundred-percent successful marriages are not achievable. We argue that humanity is broken, so it isn't realistic to think broken people can sustain relationship at that level of success. The problem with that thinking is we aren't broken anymore in Christ. He has healed us and made us new. He has secured our future and given us His Spirit to guide us. He has become our King, and we are to become members of His government. If that is all true, then why isn't marriage more successful among Christians? Paul states that marriage between a man and a woman is a picture of the kingdom, a foreshadowing of Jesus, the groom, and His glorious Bride, the body of believers. We cannot become His Bride unless we submit and align with Him. We cannot have Him and not have His government. If we really are His Bride and really want to make a statement about marriage, then we should have close to one hundred percent if not one hundred percent marriage success rate in the Body of Christ.

The institution of marriage here on Earth is to foreshadow the marriage of Jesus and His Bride, the church. I am not sure what we are waiting for. The time for glorious marriages on the earth is now. Isn't our relationship with Jesus supposed to transform every single aspect of our life from the kingdom of darkness into the kingdom of light? When is it supposed to occur? When will be a good time for Christian marriages to fulfill their calling and display the picture of Jesus and His Bride? In Heaven? Jesus said in Matthew 22:29-30, *"You are mistaken, not understanding the Scriptures nor the power of God. For in the resurrection they neither marry nor are given in marriage, but are like angels in heaven."*[4]

Jesus made it clear that marriage, as we know it here on earth, will not be similar in Heaven. There will be no need in the kingdom of Heaven to demonstrate what the union of the Savior and His Bride looks like. The union will already have taken place when Jesus returns to take His Bride. This does not mean relationships will no longer exist in Heaven. Heaven will perfect all relationships as Jesus died and rose to make all who would chose Him one with Himself, Holy Spirit, and the Father. There will be perfect unity for all eternity.

The institution of marriage here on Earth was intended by God to be a glorious demonstration of our union with Him to come. It was intended for this life to give us a taste of what the future with Him would be like. Right now, we are hard pressed to demonstrate being a Christian has any influence at all on whether a marriage is successful. We have to believe God intended for us to do better. We have to ask ourselves, if we really live from a superior kingdom, why aren't we a greater light? Where is the city on a hill that the Word of God describes?

Another key, but controversial issue related to kingdom government, alignment, authority, and submission is abortion—yes, that extremely polarizing practice which has its origins in the kingdom of darkness. You would think by any stretch of the imagination, beyond any shadow of a doubt, Christians would be opposed to abortion. Sadly, it's not true. Because of the absence of His government, alignment, and submission among Christians, abortion continues. That is not a judgment statement; it is the reality of the world we live in. God is the author of life. When we live under His government, we agree with and enable life. Only when we distort, limit, misuse, or pervert His government, do we find the taking of innocent life to be acceptable in the Body of Christ.

Somehow many Christians now believe that agreeing with abortion is an enlightened position. How will we explain that when we stand before the Almighty? How will we explain that a woman's right to choose was more important than the very plan of life itself? How will we explain our inability to live inside His boundaries, which led us to believe that abortion was an option rather than self-control and discipline? It is ever more amazing that the voice of the Body of Christ outwardly suggests she is opposed to abortion, yet her actions and the ballot box tell quite a different story. Reality shows us that abortion is just as big an issue for the church as it is for the secular community.

I have participated in many prayer gatherings, both locally and regionally, with Christians praying about ending abortion and other practices of the kingdom of darkness. I have seen a genuine cry from the Body of Christ to bring abortion to an end. I believe if we cannot stand for life, then all other issues of morality fail. If life doesn't matter, then we can all do what the Israelites in the book of Judges did. We can do, *"Whatever seemed right in [our] own eyes."*[5] What is extremely frustrating is a significant portion of these same folks come out to prayer gatherings but pull the lever for candidates that are pro-abortion when they find themselves in the voting booth. I cannot understand it.

I do know we will never see this horror defeated the way we are currently approaching it. God cannot answer a prayer for the end of abortion when many Christians are agreeing with it and giving their authority to men and women who are for abortion. It is not that He won't answer our prayer. It is that He cannot. The reality for the Body of Christ is that abortion should not be found among us. The main reason it continues to plague the Bride, again, is due to the resistance to His full government. We have not aligned and submitted to the appointed authorities in our lives. Instead, we have mingled the government of the kingdom of the world with the government of His kingdom and tried to live in both.

The results should be the same, whether the issue is marriage or any other function or subset of life. His superior kingdom should far outshine any earthly kingdom or function. What is our challenge? It is learning to live as the Bride in the King's government with alignment and submission to the King himself. Embracing the tenants of His government without alignment and submission to His government and its functions is not the answer. It again falls short of the recipe He gave us to ensure the Earth had the clearest view of His glorious Bride. We have allowed earthly kingdoms to mold our beliefs related to authority and submission. It is time we allow our minds and hearts to be reformed and transformed into His mind and His heart. This is not a new challenge. It has been a challenge from the very beginning. Even with His disciples, Jesus had to take them through many experiences to enable them to learn His heart and prepare them to be lead the government He was entrusting them with. They were to be unlike anything ever seen before on the earth, and in the book of Acts they were.

Let's take a look at some of the key revelations His disciples had to pass through in preparation for the time when they would lead the expansion of His kingdom. In the first example, Jesus has just finished telling His disciples that He is moving into the final phase of God's plan for His earthly life. He tells them that He is about to go to Jerusalem to be crucified, and that on the third day He will rise again. What is going on here? Jesus, our relational King, tells the people He is in close relationship with exactly what is about to happen. There are no smoke and mirrors, no manipulation, no softening the vision in fear that His followers are not capable of embracing it. Instead, there is great trust, honor, and love. Jesus loves His followers so dearly, He tells them just what to expect. In this moment, when He is sharing the culmination of God's glorious plan for the redemption of humanity, this is how His closest followers respond:

> *"James and John, the two sons of Zebedee, came up to Jesus, saying, 'Teacher, we want You to do for us whatever we ask of You.' And He said to them, 'What do you want Me to do for you?' They said to Him, 'Grant that we may sit, one on Your right and one on Your left, in Your glory.' But Jesus said to them, 'You do not know what you are asking. Are you able to drink the cup that I drink, or to be baptized with the baptism with which I am baptized?' They said to Him, 'We are able.' And Jesus said to them, 'The cup that I drink you shall drink; and you shall be baptized with the baptism with which I am baptized. But to sit on My right or on My left, this is not Mine to give; but it is for those for whom it has been prepared.' Hearing this, the ten began to feel indignant with James and John. Calling them to Himself, Jesus said to them, 'You know that those who are recognized as rulers of the Gentiles lord it over them; and their great men exercise authority over them. But it is not this way among*

you, but whoever wishes to become great among you shall be your servant; and whoever wishes to be first among you shall be slave of all. For even the Son of Man did not come to be served, but to serve, and to give His life a ransom for many.'" [6]

Jesus is pouring His heart out, declaring the fulfillment of all that God had promised, and all the Jews had been believing for. In this moment, His followers are arguing about who should be the greatest. This doesn't sound or look like superior kingdom behavior, does it? It looks exactly like earthly kingdom behavior. In this moment, His followers are out of alignment with what God is doing and have violated the kingdom principle of submission for their own personal need to succeed. Yes, it is true, we can make a case that wanting to be close as possible to Jesus in His heavenly kingdom is a good thing. It would be difficult to argue with the desire. What is missing here is proper alignment and submission to the vision and to the leader.

The lack of alignment and submission to Jesus opens the door to self-importance. Self-importance opens the door to division and far worse. It is probable that his followers did not intentionally decide to ignore Him when He declared His time had come. They had not matured to the level required to understand alignment and submission to the Father's plan. We are much like that today. When we do not hold honor and submission to the vision and each other in the highest regard, we open the door to all kinds of counterfeits. The inability of all His followers to understand the moment and prepare for the greatest demonstration of sacrifice and love that humanity ever witnessed results in behavior that is not at all glorious and not representative of the Kingdom.

Not only do James and John ask for something that is above and beyond what they are ready for, they are asking for something that is for the future. Jesus is trying the focus them around God's plan for now. They had no need to worry about the future. Jesus had taught them God has the future prepared for those who are in Jesus. Their request reveals their misunderstanding of their position as children of God. When we do not understand our standing in God's family, we strive for achievement. When we are not secure sons and daughters of God who are maturing into the glorious family God intended us to be, it becomes almost impossible to align and submit. We are always trying to advance and elevate ourselves, and it is always at the cost of someone else. His kingdom advances to the benefit of everyone else, not to their detriment. If we are truly governed by Him and aligned and submitted to Him, then we are an incredible blessing in every area of our life and in every circumstance we find ourselves in, no matter how difficult.

When the other ten disciples hear that James and John are trying to upstage them, it causes division, just as it would in any body of believers. It is critical to acknowledge here that this is the way the kingdoms of this world operate. Generally, in the kingdoms of this world someone else has to look bad for me to look good. Someone else has to recede so I can advance. The kingdom of Heaven is a superior kingdom. Everyone gets to advance; everyone is called to move from glory to greater glory. Jesus calls the disciples together in this instance and tells them they look just like the kingdoms of this world. He says, *"Great men of earthly kingdoms exercise authority over each other."* [7] He is speaking directly to this issue of positional authority. He says, *"It will not be that way among you."* [8] We serve a relational king and a relational kingdom. James and John are trying to secure their legacy by position. Relationship isn't secured by position, it is secured by love, honor, and covenant. *"My Kingdom does not look like that,"* Jesus says. He tells them, *"If you want to be great you must serve."*[9] What He is challenging them with is the loss of alignment with Him, what the kingdom looks like, and the inability to submit both to Him and one to another.

Here is another time when His followers did not align or submit to His vision and government. It's important to remember when Jesus tells us what drives Him, He really boils it down to two simple priorities. *"Truly, truly, I say to you, the Son can do nothing of Himself, unless it is something He sees the Father doing; for whatever the Father does, these things the Son also does in like manner."*[10] Seems so very simple. Jesus tells us clearly what drives His actions and His statements. He is completely aligned and fully submitted to the Father. He lives the model right in front of His followers. This demonstration is the fulfillment of the words He speaks in John 17:22 when He prays to the Father, *"That they [disciples] may be one just as we are one."* It is against that backdrop that we look at this next scene.

> *"When the days were approaching for His ascension, He was determined to go to Jerusalem; and He sent messengers on ahead of Him, and they went and entered a village of the Samaritans to make arrangements for Him. But they did not receive Him, because He was traveling toward Jerusalem. When His disciples James and John saw this, they said, 'Lord, do You want us to command fire to come down from heaven and consume them?' But He turned and rebuked them, and said, 'You do not know what kind of spirit you are of; for the Son of Man did not come to destroy men's lives, but to save them. And they went on to another village.'"* [11]

Jesus is on the journey toward fulfilling His destiny. This requires going to Jerusalem, where He is to offer Himself for all of humanity. He sends His followers on ahead of Him to prepare His way. He does the same today with every believer. We are called to prepare the way for Him to be known. In this account, His followers get to the next village, which is not ready to receive Him. His followers are offended. They have only one response. Their response is not from Heaven to Earth, but from Earth to Earth. The best they can think of to prepare the way for the Savior of the world is to ask Jesus if they can call fire down from Heaven and destroy this town. Reacting from an earthly kingdom always only results in damage, death, and destruction. There are so many other options available to them, yet they chose to align and submit to the kingdom of this world. They could have asked Jesus, "Can we release the greatest blessing this town has ever received?" Or, "Can we heal all the sick in this town so they will receive us?" Jesus responds to their request with a rebuke. He tells them they do not know what kind of spirit they are of. In other words, they are out of alignment and submission to the King and His kingdom.

Whenever we violate authority and submission to the vision of Heaven, we lose sight of what the Father is doing and saying. Jesus doesn't reject His disciples in these instances; He draws them back into alignment and submission to the Father's plan. His followers are learning to align and submit while walking with Him. They will not be fully aligned and submitted until Jesus is resurrected, and the Holy Spirit comes to dwell inside them. The reality for us is this is all accomplished now. The Holy Spirit hears from Him and imparts to us. The oneness that Jesus requested from the Father is now a reality if we choose it. We can now boldly affirm, "I only do and say what I see and hear Jesus do and say," because we are empowered by the Holy Spirit to do so. Yet we still do not see alignment and submission demonstrated in any grand way in the Body of Christ in a way that challenges the kingdoms of this world—at least not yet.

Let's look at one other example. The lack of kingdom government and the misuse of alignment and submission has had a very detrimental effect on the way women are treated in Christianity until very recently. I know there is much controversy on this subject, but overall it is hard to say the church has led the way when it comes to empowerment and equality for women. The reality is, we have adopted the treatment of women more from the history of earthly kingdoms than from the kingdom of Heaven. In the church culture I grew up in, the most a woman could do was teach Sunday school, serve, or perform an administrative function. The church boards and decision makers were all men, all the time. What history shows us is certain scriptures have been isolated out of context to determine what women can and cannot do. Only a few times and places were women not seen as equal to men, yet the word of God clearly states they are.

I understand men and women are different. No amount of contrived liberation will change God's grand design. However, knowing that men and women are different and are better suited to certain roles because of their differences is different than mandating that there are functions women are not allowed to perform in the kingdom. Again, when we do not embrace His full government and do not honor each function, we get distorted government and distorted outcomes. The big eruption in our culture, called the woman's liberation movement, has been fueled more by the repression and restriction of women in Christianity than by any other factor. Picture the Body of Christ operating in a way that treats, honors, and elevates women to their greatest glory possible. Think of what it could have looked like if women were already equally esteemed, paid, and regarded in

Christianity. Where would the women's liberation movement ever have had a chance to spawn? We would have and should have been leading the way in a glorious demonstration of how men and woman serve together in the superior kingdom of Heaven.

Things are changing. We are witnessing a great awakening to His government, alignment, and submission. There is much progress to be made. We still have a great resistance to alignment and submission in many parts of Christianity. I often wonder why we are not experiencing more of what God said we would and more glory than we have until now. The answer lies in coming into alignment and submission with the full government of the King. If we take a loving look at the state of the Body of Christ today, we still see too much division. We are divided around beliefs, race, age, gender, you name it—it seems we have figured out in the church how to divide into millions of splinters. We have real issues with alignment and submission. Since we have witnessed leaders in the earthly kingdoms and in the church violate principles and abuse power, we think that gives us a right to refuse to align and submit. I understand there are real cases of abusive and even corrupt leadership, and of course, in those cases we should not submit. I am speaking here to the general climate in Christianity relative to alignment and submission.

If you are a leader in the Body of Christ, it would not be uncommon to hear a believer say, "Well, I follow Jesus." Jesus appointed leaders and told them to go and appoint other leaders. Jesus leads a government and tells us, "Whoever does what I request is my follower." Saying we follow Jesus when we live outside of His full government and resist alignment and submission makes us not really followers at all. To paraphrase Jesus, "We know not what government we are of."

ENDNOTES

1. Matthew 28:18-20
2. Revelation 11:5
3. John 3:16-18
4. Matthew 22:29-30
5. Judges 21:25
6. Mark 10:35-45
7. Matthew 20:25
8. Matthew 20:26
9. Matthew 20:26
10. John 5:19-20
11. Luke 9:51-55

CHAPTER 7

IS THE MARRIAGE SUPPER TODAY?

"Then the kingdom of heaven will be comparable to ten virgins, who took their lamps and went out to meet the Bridegroom. Five of them were foolish, and five were prudent." [1]

Jesus tells us the kingdom of Heaven is comparable to ten virgins. Jesus prayed to the Father, *"Your Kingdom come, your will be done, on Earth as it is in Heaven."* [2] Who carries out the will of the Father here on earth? The Body of Christ has that responsibility, with Jesus as its head. Here again, there is a tendency in Christianity to place scriptures like the ten virgins in some future time when Christ returns. Why does He give us this revelation if it is only for the end time? Why does He give us ten virgins? Why further the division into five wise and five foolish? I believe it is directly related to government, the government of Heaven, versus a government far less glorious. Jesus tells us that ten virgins took their lamps and went out to meet the Bridegroom.

There are some very consistent themes and attributes of these ten representatives He describes. We can identify with the concept of virgins being those who are invited to the marriage of the Bridegroom. Jesus tells us He is coming back for a bride without spot or wrinkle, a bride whose virginity is restored by the sacrifice of His own blood on the cross at Calvary. The expectation of Heaven is the Bride will have the glorious nature Jesus died and rose to enable. In this case, all ten were identified as virgins. This is a statement not of individuality, but a statement of government or relationship.

Jesus tells us these ten were all on the same journey. They were all on their way to meet the Bridegroom. I think anyone who has received Jesus as his or her savior can identify with the concept of being on a journey to meet Him. It is not that we have not already met Him in the act of receiving Him; it is that our present relationship with Him is the catalyst for our ultimate destiny, which is to be with Him forever. He further tells us all ten representatives in this group had their lamps with them. In Matthew, Jesus makes this statement:

> *"You are the light of the world. A city set on a hill cannot be hidden; nor does anyone light a lamp and put it under a basket, but on the lamp stand, and it gives light to all who are in the house. Let your light shine before men in such a way that they may see your good works, and glorify your Father who is in heaven."* [3]

Jesus calls us the light of the world! What an amazing statement. I have always tended to hear this scripture as personal. But listen to what He says next: *"A city set on a hill that cannot be hidden."* [3] He is not referencing a person here, but the Body of Christ. He does not imply that His body would be hidden in the earth or blend in, but it would stand out. It would shine. Why does He use the city reference?

I believe it is directly related to government—the government of Heaven. A city with kingdom government outshines every other entity. In order for that city to shine, it has to have His government. He says, *"No one lights a lamp and puts it under a basket."* [5]

In John 1, the author states, *"Here was the true Light which, coming into the world, enlightens every man."* [6] What is the mechanism that allows our lights to come together and shine in such a way the earth is dramatically impacted? It is His presence and His government. We have put ourselves under a basket, meaning we have settled for a church government that hides the Bride, as opposed to His government, which enables the Bride to shine ever brighter. We have to go all the way back to the book of Acts to find a city we can say was a light on a hill. I do not believe it was meant to be that way, and I know cities around the world at this very moment are breaking into the glorious light He intended and are beginning to shine as bright as He always intended.

Back to the ten virgins. They are all on their way to meet the Bridegroom, and they all have a lamp. This company clearly has some relationship with Heaven and all have a lamp, meaning all are equipped to enable that city on a hill that Jesus prophesied. The light of the city is related to the good works of the Father, meaning that our lamp is tied to action. When properly governed, the Bride of Christ becomes a glorious force for good, demonstrating the kingdom of Heaven here on earth. This gets the attention of all humanity and causes them to acknowledge the glory of God. Next, Jesus does an interesting thing. After telling us the ten are all virgins and all had a lamp, He divides them and says five are wise and five are foolish. How is this possible? Why did He separate these ten when they all seemed to have the same fundamental qualifications? If they are all virgins and all have lamps, how then can they be divided? I will leave it up to God to reveal this mystery. But even though all ten had met some fundamental requirements for the journey, something was shining ever brighter for five, and something was lacking in the other five. I think the real question is why five?

I believe five is the confirmation of government. Five represents the Apostle, Prophet, Pastor, Teacher and Evangelist roles that Jesus gave to the church. I believe when the government of Heaven is fully embraced, accepted, and honored, it is full of oil. What is the significance of the oil here? For one thing, it is the fuel that keeps the lamp burning. The Bible tells us that the five wise ones had lamps full of oil, which means they had the capacity to burn the brightest for the duration of the journey. There is no question that many good things have been done by Christianity over the course of history.

There can be no argument that the world has been positively blessed by those who have dedicated their lives to Christ. Without minimizing all that we know has been accomplished, it is worth asking whether there could be more. On rare occasions and in rare places, the glory of God has broken out on the earth and Heaven touched Earth for what seemed like a moment, creating a radical shift in the earth. What we typically find when this happens is the full government of Heaven is embraced. Inevitably, they seem to dissipate almost as quickly as they arrive because we fail to embrace and sustain the government that enabled them. Christianity knows how to feed the poor and clothe the naked, and that is very important, but is that all God intended? Does the fullness of the glory of God end there? Or is there much more glory to be revealed when we align and submit to the King and His Kingdom?

"Now while the bridegroom was delaying, they all got drowsy and began to sleep. But at midnight there was a shout, 'Behold, the bridegroom!

Come out to meet him.' Then all those virgins rose and trimmed their lamps." [7] No one knows when Jesus will return. I think it's safe to say He cannot return until His Bride comes together under His government full of oil. Remember a *"city on a hill cannot be hid"* [8] and *"Let your light shine before men in such a way that they may see your good works, and glorify your Father who is in heaven."* [9] The Bride of Christ is destined to come into her own here on planet earth.

There will be no midnight in Heaven because there is no night. Midnight, when the Bride of Christ meets the Bridegroom, represents the kingdom of darkness and the kingdoms of this world. There is a midnight every single day. There is a battle between the kingdom of our God and all other kingdoms continually while we pursue His return. This, "at midnight," is not just symbolic of His future return; it is a statement about what the Bride of Christ was called to accomplish while He tarries. Notice they all became drowsy. We are not exempt from the battle with the kingdoms of this world or their impact. Victory over them can be a daily occurrence if we have the government of Heaven leading us and our lamp burning brightly. So many in Christianity are waiting for the trumpet to sound. Listen! It is already sounding. In every moment of every age. Jesus calls His Bride into the intimacy of the marriage feast so she can burn ever brighter and live ever more gloriously. For these two groups, when the call sounds to come and meet the Bridegroom, they trim their lamps. The five wise representatives of the kingdom government of Heaven had their lamps burning brightly and plenty of oil. The five unwise had no oil. Their lamps were burning out.

Why five? Why not one? Five represents His perfectly governed bride. The Body of Christ was never intended to be a group of individuals or organizations that all ran to their own beat. She was not intended to be splintered around pieces of scripture or classes of people. The

Body of Christ was always to be a glorious spectacle on the face of the planet, an accurate and grand demonstration of the glory of God. No individual works independently in God's kingdom. She is a bride with all members intricately fit together. She is a peculiar group of people who thinks of herself as glorious and everyone else as just as glorious, or even more so.

When the Bridegroom is announced, all the virgins awake to trim their lamps. I believe the Body of Christ is awakening to the call of the Bridegroom. She, His bride, is beginning to embrace the fullness of the government her King died to give her. She is learning to embrace all the offices of His government, not just by accepting them but also by honoring them. She recognizes that without the King's government, there is no chance she can fully develop the glory He intended for her to display here on earth.

The state of Christianity in recent history is very deeply influenced by individuality, whether it be personal, a people group, a nationality, or a denomination. A sense of "pioneer-ism," that is primarily a western culture trait resists submission and alignment. This attitude tends to divide on issues rather than unify in relationship. Get around believers and you will often hear the statement, "Jesus would have died for even one person." I am sure He would have, but He didn't, and never intended to. God's heart has always been that no one should be lost. Our salvation is not just for us—it is for the whole Earth to see His glory revealed as we come together as His body to demonstrate His goodness. When we as saints are governed in a way that matures us only as individuals, as opposed to a body of believers, we have been governed poorly. We have not been governed in a way which matures us from children to glorious adults, to mature saints, demonstrating the fullness of Christ and the love of God, fully equipped for works of service. These works of service are instances of Heaven touching earth. Only the government Jesus gave us in its fullness can enable this Body of Christ.

"The foolish said to the prudent, 'Give us some of your oil, for our lamps are going out.' But the prudent answered, 'No, there will not be enough for us and you too; go instead to the dealers and buy some for yourselves'." [10] Both groups arise and get their lamps burning. Both groups are surely on their way to meet the Bridegroom. Most of Christianity desires to meet the Bridegroom. We talk about this scripture as though it is an end-time event and there will be a future meeting when believers for all ages meet the Bridegroom. But what about today and what of tomorrow? What of every day that anyone seeks to enter into His presence? Is that not meeting the Bridegroom? Is that not attending the marriage supper of the lamb? Did Jesus not say in John 6:35, *"I am the bread of Life. He who comes to me will never hunger and he who believes in me will never thirst,"*? Is this not a call to the marriage supper on a daily basis? It cannot be argued that Jesus is only talking about the end times or judgment day when He makes this statement. Is it not necessary to be in relationship with Him to see His glory revealed on the earth? What is the culture that facilitates propelling the saints into a marriage supper experience with the Bridegroom every day? It is that of the apostle, prophet, pastor, teacher, and evangelist all governing in unity and propelling the saints into their place at the marriage supper.

The five who have little oil ask the five who have much oil to give them some. I believe the abundance of oil is the value, honor, and respect that the five wise carried for the government of Heaven. In essence, it is the glorious overflow of believers maturing under the full government of Heaven. They walked in the fullness of their own calling in the government. They are also understood to be totally prepared and shining bright to defeat the darkness and meet the Bridegroom every day, and they need each function of the government. The five foolish have little oil. They have little reverence for the importance and necessity of the government of Heaven as the enabler of the flow of oil. Without a constant flow of oil, the light cannot shine in the darkness and we cannot meet the Bridegroom. The five wise tell the five foolish they could not give them oil.

There has to be sacrifice to have a bride full of oil. There has to be the government of Heaven propelling the saints into the marriage supper of the lamb every day. We have many good plans, intentions, and actions. On a daily basis, however, the earth is intended to be experiencing the Bride of Christ in a tangible, supernatural way. That is not the case today, at least not to the degree I believe it was meant to be. We only have to look around at the culture to see that Christianity at large is more like any other group rather than a Glorious Bride meeting and living from that marriage supper with the Bridegroom.

"And while they were going away to make the purchase, the bridegroom came, and those who were ready went in with him to the wedding feast; and the door was shut."[11] The Bride of Christ is destined to intimacy with the Bridegroom every day. That was, and is, God's plan for the Bride on the earth. For the Bride to radiate the glory of God, she has to attend the marriage supper of the Lamb daily. The Bride, when properly governed, is full of oil and burning brightly on display for the entire world to observe. As she enters into the marriage supper of the Lamb, she brings Heaven to Earth in healing, freedom, miracles, and all the wonders of Heaven. As she matures in this daily intimacy, she becomes more aware of what happens in Heaven and more desperate to see Heaven on earth.

It is behind that shut door, daily at the marriage supper of the Lamb, that the Bride gets ever more spectacular and continues to radically impact the earth with the King's glory. The five wise, representing the Bride who is governed from Heaven, had more than enough oil to hear the call at midnight and enter in. Her motive is never selfish or narrow. Just like God himself, His bride enlarges her heart daily for all to see and experience the heart of the Father and Heaven here on Earth. The five foolish, those not governed well, have limited oil and not enough to get them through midnight and into the marriage supper. These are not burning brightly and are not marked differently from the kingdoms of this world. They have knowledge because they have some oil but have reduced His government to match their intentions rather than embracing His government to accomplish His intentions.

Those with limited oil are encouraged to go and buy from sellers. The Bride cannot buy the glory that Jesus gave Himself for her to carry. She has to mature into it. She has to grow in a government that embodies all five of the functions that Jesus gifted her. It is not something to be obtained in a single prayer or a one-time miracle. It is a deliberate maturing occurring to the body of believers who have made Christ their head and His government their covering. It can't be obtained by vote, tradition, or edict. This heaven-governed bride only comes about by intention and experience over time. The five foolish find themselves in panic mode. The fact that it is midnight pressures them into having a solution when they find themselves short. They are pressed by time, lack, and the impossibility of the moment. Their knowledge will not propel them in this moment. Good management and gifts are not enough. Oil is the missing ingredient, and it represents fullness. It is the fullness of government and relationship with both God and man.

In sharp contrast, the five wise are ready; they have solutions, hope, and anticipation. They are not looking to escape or survive. They are burning brightly, creating a great phenomenon in the earth. They have intentionally embraced the government of Heaven because they are convinced their King has the answers, the healings, and all the heavenly goodness humanity desperately needs. They are not looking to escape the earth for a mansion in Heaven; they are wholeheartedly believing God has a glorious plan for humanity which has not been fulfilled. Every day's midnight brings another opportunity for the Bride of Christ to be an ever more glorious force on the planet. *"Later the other virgins also came, saying, 'Lord, Lord, open up for us' But he answered, 'Truly I say to you, I do not know you'."* [12]

The five who went to buy came back. Somehow, they were able to find the door. Interestingly enough, it does not say they had obtained oil. I believe with all my heart there was still a resistance to the government of Heaven. Had these five repented, turned their hearts, and embraced Heaven's government, I believe He would have opened the door. Remember when Jesus said *"Not everyone who says to Me, 'Lord, Lord,' will enter the kingdom of heaven, but he who does the will of My Father who is in heaven will enter"?* [13] Pay specific attention to Jesus' words. He says, *"will enter the Kingdom of Heaven,"* not *"will be saved."* The kingdom has a government, and if we cannot embrace the government He has gifted us on earth, how can we expect to enter His heavenly government? If the government is on His shoulders, how can we see Heaven here on Earth if we do not embrace and submit to His government? The Bride of Christ has for far too long been governed in a way that is not full of oil. This fullness of oil is not something that can be obtained; it has to be received. Jesus has gifted to His bride a government. His government was intended to nurture a bride who would always be full of oil.

The door was shut. The door is the intersection of Heaven and earth. The invitation to intimacy and the marriage supper of the Lamb is a standing invitation. It is available to the Bride of Christ at His call. It is a necessary relationship if the Bride is to shine as brightly as she should. The door only opens at His call, but He is always calling.

> *"Behold, I stand at the door and knock; if anyone hears My voice and opens the door, I will come in to him and will dine with him, and he with Me. He who overcomes, I will grant to him to sit down with Me on My throne, as I also overcame and sat down with My Father on His throne."* [14]

Jesus has an open-door policy. The issue is, we cannot enter to dine with Him when we do not possess His government. He grants that he who overcomes will sit with Him on His throne. We typically apply this scripture around a person and not the Bride. Jesus here is speaking to the church—His Bride. He is not calling individuals, He is calling His bride to come and dine with Him. Yes, of course, we accept Him individually, but the invitation is into a family, a body, a glorious company of relational humans who effortlessly reproduce the relational glory displayed by the Father, Son, and Holy Spirit. Nor is this a one-time invitation. It is a standing invitation to come into intimacy with Him. It is the Bride of Christ when governed as God intended that can overcome and sit with Him on His throne. Is that for then or for now? It is for both then and now. Unfortunately, for much of history, the Body of Christ has been taught it is for *then only*. The door is shut to the five who have no oil with which to overcome. They do not have a government enabling them to shine as a city on a hill—no government that can overcome. The Bride of Christ is greater than any entity on earth. She is to be a company of every tribe and tongue, astonishing the kingdoms of this world with her glory, the glory of the Bridegroom, a glory that is continuously increasing as she attends the marriage supper of the Lamb daily.

The five with no oil come back and ask to be let in. Notice they came as they did originally, as a group of five. There is great significance in the number five both for those who enter in, and those who do not. There is much conversation in the Body of Christ today about the five-fold government, but conversation and implementation are entirely different. There is much anticipation growing for the government of Heaven, a government that is full of oil. None of them came to the door as an individual and said, "Open up for me." This speaks directly to the necessity of the five offices of government. These were virgins, just like the five wise. They were on the same journey as the others, but the difference is they did not embrace the heart or fullness of His government.

Jesus responds to the call saying, *"I do not know you."* How can this be? Were they not virgins like the others? Were their intentions not good? Didn't they hear the call at midnight just like the others? What went wrong? What was missing? We have to carefully re-examine centuries of behavior in the Body of Christ and understand we have access to much more than we have experienced. We are not smarter or more deserving than our forefathers. Jesus has always been calling His bride to shine in the fullness of His glory. In the church's zeal to protect knowledge and establish orthodoxy, it has prevented revelation of greater glory down through the centuries. Beyond the early church of Acts, the Bride through the ages has protected some truths of the kingdom at the expense of the greater glory Jesus died to give her. Along the way, she has lost focus and adapted to worldly kingdom government at the expense of the government of Heaven, which produces a city on a hill.

"Be on the alert then, for you do not know the day nor the hour." [15] Jesus, after telling the five foolish they are not known, says to be on alert, for we do not know the day nor the hour. What is He saying? What

does it mean to be on the alert? I believe it means be full of oil; be governed in the fullness of the government that He died to give to His bride. This government nurtures, guides, and propels saints into their maturity and a unity that produces a fantastic demonstration here on earth. Read the book of Acts again. See how the infant Bride of Christ so radiated His glory that they turned the world upside down. See a group of believers walking together in commonality, meeting each other's needs, and performing the works of the kingdom of Heaven here on earth. Many will say this was just a period of time where God wanted to establish His church, so He extended greater grace during that season. Do not believe it. God is the same yesterday, today, and forever. What happened in the book of Acts and the early church was just the beginning of what was intended to be an ever-greater blessing to mankind, the manifestation of the Bride of Christ. The Bride became sidetracked. She started to grow and move in her own independence. She mixed parts of the Heavenly kingdom with secular kingdoms and settled for organized religion instead of ever-increasing, organic kingdom glory.

Be on the alert. In other translations, it says to *watch*. What is the implication? Are we so detached from His plan for humanity we do not realize every day is the day, and every hour is the hour? How can we claim to have intimacy with Him and not know our place, not know that we are seated in heavenly places? How can we say we are seated in heavenly places with Him and not produce a heavenly impact here on the earth? Watch. I wonder if over the many centuries we have become so preoccupied with what the devil is doing and what the kingdom of darkness is up to that we have missed the daily marriage supper of the Lamb. Our unwillingness to embrace all He intended for us has conditioned the Bride of Christ to set herself apart, to retreat from the culture as opposed to defining it. Is it possible the devil has so much influence because the Bride of Christ has been living in hiding, hoping to be rescued? Many Christians are living for His return so they can escape this life, not realizing when we feast with Him daily at the marriage supper of the Lamb, He enables us to be the overcomers the planet needs to see.

We are sometimes more like the scribes and Pharisees then we are the Bride. Jesus said to the religious people of His day, "You search the Scriptures because you think that in them you have eternal life; it is these that testify about Me."[16] They were experts in the word and oral tradition, yet they could not receive the Savior they were so intent on finding when He was in their midst. They were so intent on protecting what had been given to them they could not receive what was prepared for them. They could not receive what was necessary for the moment and beyond because past experience limited their ability to grow. I do not at all believe they were inherently or intentionally evil. I do believe they had governed themselves into a glory-less theology and existence. In Matthew 23:27 Jesus laments over Jerusalem, the representative of the Bride in His day. He declares the inability of His people to receive the prophets, most specifically Himself, and the revelation God has intended for them. He agonizes over the Bride's inability to unite under Him and His government, around God's grand purpose for humanity. He tells them they will not see Him until they recognize Him and His reign and say. *"Blessed is He who comes in the name of the Lord."* [17]

The Bride of Christ has spent much of history since Jesus ascended focused on what the kingdom of darkness and Satan is doing, as opposed to what she was called to do and be in every generation. Jesus says, *"Watch therefore for you do not know the day or the hour."* [18] This means we do not know the day of His final return. He has also told us He is with us always, and when we dine with Him, we overcome. We do not have to know the time or the day. If we are dining with

Him daily and functioning in the fullness of His government, full of oil, that day will be no surprise to His bride. She will hear the final call, and her lamp will be brighter than it has ever been because she has been ever-increasing. In the meantime, she is to watch that she is ever maturing, ever more glorious, ever brighter.

Go out and talk to believers anywhere. You will get more believers telling you how evil and dark the world is becoming than you will how glorious and incredible the church is becoming. It doesn't mean we are to be ignorant of the enemy and the kingdom of darkness. Satan is real, and his only focus is to kill, steal and destroy. When we focus our energy and passion on watching Him and what He is doing, we lose sight of the Father and what He wants to do. We lose hope for humanity and for tomorrow. We take pieces of the scripture like 1 Peter 5:8: *"the devil, prowls around like a roaring lion, seeking someone to devour"* to develop our lives and futures around. Instead of overflowing with oil, we find our lamps are going dim and we have to ask to borrow oil from others. We develop an "us versus them" mentality and crowd in on ourselves. We allow ourselves to be governed in ways that validate our skewed theology, rather than aligning ourselves and submitting to the government of Heaven, a government gifted to us by Jesus himself.

We need a government that stretches, pushes, elevates, and propels us out of self-validating theology into mature saints united in love and bursting with the fullness of the works that God has prepared for the Bride to release on the earth. She's coming. The Bride is finding herself and beginning to realize her destiny and inheritance. All over the planet the Bride is awakening and embracing all of the government Jesus has gifted her. She is in the wedding planning stage of life and there has never been a greater time to be alive!

ENDNOTES

1. Matthew 25:1-2
2. Matthew 6:10
3. Matthew 5:14-16
4. Matthew 5:14
5. Matthew 5:15
6. John 1:9
7. Matthew 25:5-7
8. Matthew 5:14
9. Matthew 5:16
10. Matthew 25:8-9
11. Matthew 25:10
12. Matthew 25:11-12
13. Matthew 7:21-23
14. Revelation 3:20-21
15. Matthew 25:13
16. John 5:39
17. Matthew 23:39
18. Matthew 25:13

CHAPTER 8
THE BRIDE MADE READY

> *"'Let us rejoice and be glad and give the glory to Him, for the marriage of the Lamb has come and His bride has made herself ready.' It was given to her to clothe herself in fine linen, bright and clean; for the fine linen is the righteous acts of the saints. Then he said to me, 'Write, 'Blessed are those who are invited to the marriage supper of the Lamb.'" And he said to me, 'These are true words of God.'"*[1]

We started out with this scripture, and we will finish with it. What an incredible picture we are given in Revelation of what the Bride of Christ looks like. Chapter 19 starts out with an amazing description of the sight and sound of the happenings in Heaven as His bride is celebrated. High praise is given to God, for He has judged the great harlot and avenged the blood of His servants. A great multitude in Heaven, along with the four living creatures and the twenty-four elders, enter into an all-out worship session for what God has accomplished. There is much excitement, recognition, praise, and celebration over what God has done, building up to the announcement of the marriage of the Lamb. More importantly, it is a level of excitement not really imaginable by our human faculties concerning one thing, the Bride of Christ who has made herself ready.

If we could get greater revelation about how Heaven celebrates His bride, we could see changes in the Earth that have never before been witnessed. Generally, the Body of Christ understands this to be an end-time celebration, some event to take place in the future, maybe after the day of judgment, but certainly after the world ends. I do not believe this to be the case at all. I did believe that way for a significant part of my life, but I realize now I believed that way because of what I was taught and how I was governed.

It is clear from His Word there is a constant celebration in the Kingdom of Heaven as all the elders, angels, and saints celebrate the victory God gave us through the sacrifice and resurrection of Jesus, our Bridegroom. All of Heaven looks on continually to recognize and celebrate the Bride's freedom, enabled by her loving Bridegroom. In Luke 15:7, we are told there is great joy over one sinner who repents. Imagine the intensity of the joy and celebration when all of Heaven looks down upon the entire Bride of Christ. Is this a daily happening as we know it, based on time in days as measured here on earth? I don't think so. I think it's fair to say we do not know how time is measured in the kingdom of Heaven, but it is also fair to say this is not a one-time event. It is clear for every day in earthly time that God extends the grace He gifted to humanity in the form of His Son. This same celebration continues as all of Heaven adores the Bride and her glory here on the earth. It makes me think about Hebrews chapter 11, in which the great cloud of witnesses is gathered and cheering on the saints here on Earth to come into the full revelation of their inheritance as the Bride of Christ.

"Let us rejoice and be glad and give the glory to Him, for the marriage of the Lamb has come and His bride has made herself ready." [2] We are told that this great multitude, with its magnificent voice, is worshiping God for the marriage of the Lamb has come. There is great anticipation in Heaven for His bride to enter daily into the marriage supper, for it is in this place of intimacy and relationship that the bride grows ever more glorious and shines ever brighter the glory of God on the earth. This great voice resounding throughout Heaven says, *"His bride has made herself ready!"* What a proclamation! What a fascinating sight! Why are the hosts of Heaven so excited, so passionate? They understand all that God has gifted to the church, His bride, enabling her to be the phenomenon she was intended to be here on the earth. They long for the day the Bride herself will come into the fullness of this same revelation.

This is beginning to happen. There has been a great awakening in the Body of Christ for many decades now. It has been building for some time. There is a level of maturity bursting forth as the Bride begins to reconnect with her destiny and prepare herself for her Bridegroom. There is great revelation being received by many in the body that the wedding supper of the lamb is not just a future event or an event we get to attend when we pass from this life to the next, but it is an event happening now. It is today and every day that all the host of Heaven anticipate and celebrate the Bride making herself ready to attend the marriage supper of the Lamb. It is today and every day until Jesus returns that the Bride of Christ owes humanity a demonstration of the glory of God that can only be realized when the Bride attends the marriage supper daily. The Bride can only attend the marriage supper of the Lamb daily when she is governed by His government.

His bride has made herself ready. This sounds like such an odd statement. For so much of history the Church has been governed and taught that Jesus makes us ready. As long as we accept Him as our Savior, the rest will be worked out by Him. Think about all the challenges on the Earth right now, and ask yourself if the Bride is ready for the marriage supper. Am I, as part of the Bride, ready for the marriage supper? If we see this only in the context of salvation, then we can respond we are ready. However, if we challenge ourselves about what we are to be ready for, we may have to answer differently. We are to be daily demonstrating the glory of Heaven's King and His kingdom here on earth. It is a radical shift for Christianity in the way we think, believe, and behave. It will also produce a radical shift in the earth. It will free us from our survivor mentality and propel us into a glorious future when the King and His kingdom bring healing, restoration, providence, and hope to humanity through a bride who has made herself ready. It is compelling that He does not say that God, Jesus, or Holy Spirit has made the Bride ready, but that she herself has made herself ready. How is that possible? What can the Bride do beyond accepting Jesus to make herself ready?

She has to embrace His government. When Jesus was before Pontius Pilate this exchange occurred:

> *"Therefore, Pilate entered again into the Praetorium, and summoned Jesus and said to Him, 'Are You the King of the Jews?' Jesus answered, 'Are you saying this on your own initiative, or did others tell you about Me?' Pilate answered, 'I am not a Jew, am I? Your own nation and the chief priests delivered You to me; what have You done?' Jesus answered, 'My kingdom is not of this world. If My kingdom were of this world, then My servants would be fighting so that I would not be handed over to the Jews; but as it is, my kingdom is not of this realm.'"*[3]

Pilate questions Jesus as to whether He is a king. Jesus responds that His kingdom is not of this world. It's a superior kingdom. It is a kingdom of glory, healing, miracles, and freedom. Jesus says, "If my kingdom were of this realm, then my servants would fight." He meant if all His kingdom produced was the same as the earthly kingdoms, then we would battle in the earthly realm. However, the kingdom of God is a superior kingdom with a superior outcome to be experienced in superior way in every facet of life. His kingdom doesn't produce war; it produces peace. It doesn't produce sickness; it produces health. It produces life and not death.

It is under His kingdom's government that the Bride makes herself ready. His bride is currently coming into an awareness of the lack in her own readiness. She is now maturing to the point where she can no longer accept the government of earthly kingdoms to advance Heaven's plans. She is realizing her inheritance and her destiny to be ready daily to demonstrate the glory of the King for all humanity to see. She has awakened to the need for His government to guide her and enable her to shine far brighter than she has ever believed possible until this time in history.

Similarly, when Jesus appeared to His followers after He was resurrected, He had this exchange with them:

> *"So when they had come together, they were asking Him, saying, 'Lord, is it at this time You are restoring the kingdom to Israel.' He said to them, 'It is not for you to know times or epochs which the Father has fixed by His own authority; but you will receive power when the Holy Spirit has come upon you; and you shall be My witnesses both in Jerusalem, and in all Judea and Samaria, and even to the remotest part of the earth.'"*[4]

His followers are looking for Him to restore and reign in an earthly kingship. Jesus, through His coming, dying, and rising again, has ushered in a new season, a new time and covenant. It is a time for Heaven on earth. It is now a time when all who receive Him and His government will receive power to bring Heaven here on earth. Earthly kingdoms, the kingdoms of this world, cannot produce glory because they are fading and will one day all bow to His kingdom. For far too long, the Church has been seeking the re-establishment of a substandard kingdom, but God has given us all we need to establish a superior kingdom. *"You will receive power when Holy Spirit is upon you to be witnesses all over the earth."* [5] Witnesses to what? To a superior King and a superior kingdom. Not to a tradition or a doctrine, but to the kingdom of Heaven. A kingdom whose government is ever-increasing, expanding, and more glorious.

Let's look closely at how His bride has made herself ready. It says that His bride clothed herself, meaning she put on the garments of fine linen. She took action. She made herself ready by submitting to His government. She embraced all God gifted her to propel the saints into their destiny. She is filled with acts of His heavenly kingdom. This is directly tied to Ephesians 4:11-12. When Paul announces to the Body of Christ that Jesus died and gifted us the governmental structure that enables the Bride to live as spectacularly as possible, he immediately tells us why Heaven's government is necessary. It is necessary to equip the saints for works of service.

Look at how the Bride has made herself ready in Revelation 19. She does so by clothing herself in the righteous acts of the saints. What is it that enables the righteous acts of the saints? It is the government Jesus gifted us, a government that brings Heaven to earth. The government of Heaven is not something that can be built or earned. Just like salvation, it has to be received. The Bride must come to an awareness that though she is redeemed (a virgin), in order for her to make herself fully ready, she has to embrace His government. His government leads from the bottom up. His government serves the saints and humanity and enables saints in their acts of the kingdom by spreading the glory of God across the earth. His government is relational—as Father, Son, and Holy Spirit are one, so the government of Heaven is meant to be one. Five offices working together to enable the saints and build up the maturity and unity of the Bride, each office of government honoring and dependent on each of the other offices. This government is unlike any we have seen in the natural realm, one that provokes jealousy and awe by all who observe it. Habakkuk 2:14 states: *"For the earth will be filled with the knowledge of the glory of the Lord, as the waters cover the sea."*

This is not a day we have seen. The time is now. It is now the Bride is coming into her own. It is now she realizes independence, popularity, recognition, and isolation will not produce the glory of Heaven nor allow the Bride to get herself fully ready. It is now she understands gifting alone is not enough. Many gifted Christians have left their mark on history. Jesus is coming for His bride, not just a gifted individual. He is looking for a bride glowing in the garments of the works of the saints, a company aligned and submitted to His government. This company is so glorious it provokes the culture to jealousy. We have settled for much less glory than God intended by adapting to culture, as opposed to defining it. We have adopted government principles from inferior kingdoms as opposed to receiving and accepting Heaven's government. We have lamented the decline of the culture and the decline of Christian influence in all segments of the culture, yet it is the government of Heaven that enables the Bride to restore the culture.

Let's look at how the prophet Isaiah describes the bride in Isaiah 60:1-7:

> *"Arise, shine; for your light has come, and the glory of the Lord has risen upon you. For behold, darkness will cover the earth and deep darkness the peoples; But the Lord will rise upon you and His glory will appear upon you. Nations will come to your light, and kings to the brightness of your rising. Lift up your eyes round about and see; they all gather together, they come to you. Your sons will come from afar, and your daughters will be carried in the arms. Then you will see and be radiant, and your heart will thrill and rejoice; because the abundance of the sea will be turned to you, the wealth of the nations will come to you. A multitude of camels will cover you, the young camels of Midian and Ephah; all those from Sheba will come; they will bring gold and frankincense, and will bear good news of the praises of the Lord. All the flocks of Kedar will be gathered together to you, the rams of Nebaioth will minister to you; they will go up with acceptance on My altar, and I shall glorify My glorious house."*

It is amazing how the prophet describes the Bride. Arise and shine! Sounds just like the scripture Matthew 5 that says, *"Let your light so shine before men so they may see your good works and glorify your Father who is in Heaven."* Isaiah is describing the Glorious Bride, the Bride we read about in Revelation, who is governed with Heaven's government, clothed in the garments which are the works of the saints, and attends the marriage supper of the Lamb daily. He describes the time that the Bride would shine, when darkness covers the earth and a deep darkness covers the people. This is the time for the Bride to awaken to her destiny. Light shines greater in deeper darkness.

The Lord will rise upon you, and His glory will appear upon you. We are in a time when darkness is great, but there is a greater hunger in the church for His presence. We have a building sense that we were meant for more than we have been governed into. Much of the Body of Christ has a great sense that Heaven's government is necessary for Him to rise upon the Bride. There is great anticipation for impacting the culture by bringing Heaven to earth, and much is being currently written and taught about how to influence sectors of the culture. It all flows from the foundation of His government. Where His government has been accepted, embraced, and honored, we are seeing amazing changes in cities and the culture.

"Nations will come to your light and kings to the brightness of your rising."[6] Wow! Has that happened yet on the earth? The Bride is intended to be glorious in everything she does, not religious, but glorious. She is to be displaying such incredible light that nations and kings come running to see her splendor. Remember Solomon. He had such wisdom that the glory of God was on everything he did, even the way he set up his palace. Kings and dignitaries came to observe all the glory that rose upon Israel because of Solomon's hunger to embrace Heaven's government. The demonstration of the Glorious Bride occurs anytime and anywhere God's government is embraced. We are moving toward this great realization in our time.

The nations and kings of the Earth are in turmoil, there continue to be wars and rumors of wars, and there are great economic and environmental challenges. The nations and kings of the Earth are looking for answers. They are looking for a light shining brightly. His Bride has seemed indifferent and detached, driven by a theology of defeat rather than victory. Not any more! His bride is awakening. She is remembering her inheritance and destiny. She has looked back at her life and has seen all too often she attempted to exist in her own strength, functioning from gifting, governed by earthly principles and concepts, rather than the King's government.

As the Bride renews covenant with the King and His kingdom, she is rapidly increasing the oil in her lamp. As a result, she is burning ever brighter and moving into a time when a great harvest will come due to those attracted by her light. Her light will be the works and wonders of Heaven released here on Earth for the benefit of humanity. She is entering into a time of intense preparation for the great wedding feast and is involved daily in the dress rehearsal of the marriage supper.

She will not be known by a denomination or tradition, but by the radiance of God flowing from her company. Romans 8:19 states: *"For the anxious longing of the creation waits eagerly for the revealing of the sons of God."*

This is true for every generation, and we have only witnessed it in part. There has always been, and will always be, a great longing for the revelation of God's glory. This is stronger now than at any time history. Increasing wealth, knowledge, and technology have not filled the intense need of humanity and creation to experience the intense glory of God. We are rapidly moving into a time where all of creation will observe the Glorious Bride in all of her splendor, walking in unity, power, and love, bringing Heaven to Earth and satiating the groans of all humanity and creation. The wealth of the nations will come to her, and she will justly and rightly divide and bless humanity in a way the has not occurred on the planet since the early church in the book of Acts. She will no longer look to escape the world or to judge the world, but like Her king before her, she will serve the world in splendor and glory.

Isaiah is not speaking about Heaven but about events here on earth. I do not believe he is speaking about a millennial time, but he is giving us a prophetic picture of what the Bride was always intended to look like. The government of Heaven as Paul reveals to us in Ephesians 4 has always been in force. It is all over the Bible, both Old and New Testaments. Prior to Jesus, it was veiled as God governed through people like Abraham and Moses. For example, the people told Moses in Exodus 20:19: *"Speak to us yourself and we will listen; but let not God speak to us, or we will die."* Jesus tore the veil and revealed the fullness of the government of Heaven so that the Bride could be God's glorious representative in the earth.

Let's look at one other time in history the government of Heaven was necessary to ensure victory and demonstrate God's glory. This is part of the history of King David. It is found in 1 Samuel 17. David has recently been anointed king while he is still the least of his family and performing the role of shepherd. The Philistines, the enemies of the Israelites, have come to battle against them. We find a challenge by Goliath, the Philistine leader, to the Israelites to come out and fight him, and the winner's kingdom will rule.

There is only one superior kingdom, and that is the kingdom of Heaven. Whenever we try to sustain ourselves or advance ourselves without His government, we also wind up being taunted by inferior kingdoms. It is no different today. We cannot see the fullness of the Bride without the fullness of His government. The Israelites are in fear, unable to find anyone to stand up to Goliath. King Saul himself is not willing to fight him. Day after day, Goliath comes out to taunt the Israelite army and their king.

David is sent by his father to bring supplies to his brothers on the battle lines. When David arrives, he hears Goliath mocking the

Israelite army. He volunteers to fight for his king. David had a great history with God because he had cultivated intimacy with God and had experienced bringing Heaven to Earth by defeating a lion and a bear. David walked in submission and alignment with what God was doing and allowed God to reveal to him Heaven's ways. Even though he is anointed king, he does not go to the battle lines this day as king, but as servant. He is willing to do what is right in front of him and trust God to work out the rest.

When David hears Goliath mocking the people of God, his zeal for God's honor and his understanding that he is a member of a superior kingdom rises up in him. David declares that he will fight and demonstrates he is a representative of a superior kingdom.

It is interesting to note at the time of this battle, we know that David had been anointed king but is not yet king. Later, as we look back at David's life, we can see every one of the five governmental offices flowing out of his life. It is clear that the strongest anointing is of the apostolic and prophetic. As David arrives at the battle line to bring food and supplies to his brothers, he discerns the assault on the kingdom of God. He recognizes it is impossible for an inferior kingdom with an inferior government to stand against God and the superior government of Heaven. Even his own brothers mock him and accuse him of false motives, but David understands Heaven's government.

David is brought to King Saul and told he is too small and too inexperienced to encounter such a battle. This is so relevant today. We are taunted by the culture and the assault on the kingdom of Heaven and God's purposes. It appears to be certain defeat. It seems like no one will stand for battle. There are many, however, who, like David, understand Heaven's government and their ranks are expanding rapidly in this season. Saul realizes he cannot convince David not to fight and offers to provide his armor. This, again, is a picture of the Bride of Christ choosing to adapt ill-fitting armor for the battle with the kingdoms of this world instead of choosing the government of Heaven.

David attempts to wear the armor. The Bride, over the course of the centuries, has tried different armor. It has provided some protection and won some battles, but she has now come to the realization in this age that the armor and the tactics of earthly kingdoms are inferior. She is rapidly developing the maturity she was destined for as she prepares to meet the Bridegroom daily. Only Heaven's government will allow her to thrive and war in the splendor of Heaven that defeats all inferior governments.

David refuses to fight in someone else's armor. The Bride has decided to fight from her position in Heaven's government seated in Heavenly places with Christ Jesus. David takes off the armor of Saul and says, "I cannot fight in this, I have not tested it." What a statement. The Body of Christ for too long has tried to fight in armor that it has not tested. This means the armor was not fit for the Bride. She could not win in ill-fitting armor.

David leaves Saul and he proceeds to a brook. With his stick in hand, he chooses five smooth stones. The brook, in this instance, represents a prophetic picture of the river of life. It is a glimpse of that glorious river that brings healing and restoration to the nations. The river itself carries the government of Heaven in it and is flowing with redemption, victory, and all that humanity so desperately needs. The government of Heaven increases the flow of the river. They go hand-in-hand. The government of Heaven enables the flow, and the flow carries government to the nations.

David chooses the government of Heaven to represent him in battle with an inferior kingdom. It is no surprise. David had a history with Heaven. He spent time with God and understood the value of God's government. He had the revelation that no kingdom could stand against the kingdom of the Almighty.

What do the five smooth stones represent? They represent the apostolic, prophetic, pastoral, teaching, and evangelistic functions of Heaven's government. They aren't just stones, they are smooth stones. That is very important because it symbolizes these offices working seamlessly together to enable the fullness of God's government and the glory and victory that come with it. They represent the oneness of relationship among the five and the absence of independence, superiority, competition, division, and selfishness. David, with his sling, is given the incredible opportunity to propel the government of God towards the inferior government of the enemy. He is God's agent for ensuring victory for his people.

David certainly represents the apostolic and prophetic in this battle. He sees Heaven's vision for the people of Israel and declares that no enemy can stand against the God of Heaven. He sees the blueprint of what God wants to do. David is not sidetracked by fear, he is not overcome by circumstance, and he does not let his lack of position or title prevent him from executing Heaven's plan. Many in the Body of Christ right now, and more who are coming, fit this same description. They are not people of position or title, but they are people filled with the desperate hunger to see the blueprint of the Bride full of glory emerge upon the planet. They are people who have cultivated a deep relationship with Jesus in the quiet places. They've achieved great intimacy with God in the day-to-day battles. Having moved into a place of revelation, they know there is a rapid maturing happening in the Bride of Christ, and she is about to stun the world with the greatest demonstration of God's presence and glory that it has ever seen.

David ignores the mocking of Goliath and tells him he would be defeated so all the world would know the God of Heaven. The mandate has never changed. It has been God's intention since creation that man and woman, his most glorious creations, would be the picture of God here on the earth. Sin broke that covenant but Jesus came, died, and resurrected to restore us to God's image and transform us from sinners to saints. David declares that the battle is the Lord's, and He always wins. Upon this declaration, he runs toward the enemy. The Bride of Christ today is beginning to accelerate toward the enemy, the kingdoms of the world. After many centuries of retreat, isolation, judgment, division, and hand-wringing, the Bride has come into her own.

She is no longer willing to sit by as the enemy destroys souls and plunders cities. She has awakened to her destiny and is coming into a great time of advance where she will run at the enemy's kingdoms of the world and make them the kingdoms of our God. She is casting off tradition and false humility and taking her rightful place, seated in heavenly places with Christ Jesus. She is no longer content to believe that her Bridegroom will come and rescue her from the depraved world. She understands now more than ever before she was meant to war for all the victory Jesus purchased on the cross. She was meant to give the world a tangible experience with Heaven here on earth. She was meant to be the most hopeful, loving, creative, splendid, beautiful, and resourceful company of people ever observed on the earth. She was meant to meet her Bridegroom on that fateful day as a glorious victor, who by all that her Bridegroom had done for her, presents Him with countless victories. She will present her Bridegroom with city after city and nation after nation of light burning bright with the glory of the Lord.

David ran toward the enemy, reaches into his sling, and pulls out one stone. I believe it is the apostolic stone. It is the apostolic office that sees what God and Heaven see, and then puts it in motion here on earth. It is David's call to set in motion the blueprint of Heaven. It is key that he has all five stones. He could have just chosen one or two. He didn't. He chooses five. He chooses five for a reason. It takes all five governmental offices to enable the Bride to be and do all Jesus has prepared for her.

He understands that with the five stones, he carries the complete functional government of Heaven with Him. In reality, no matter which stone he chooses, the victory is ensured, because the victory comes with the government. How many battles have we seen in the natural in which because of a lack of fullness of Heaven's government, victory has not been sustainable? How many victories in the Body of Christ have been unsustainable because Heaven's government was not fully embraced? How many great revivals and great moves of God have dried up because the government of Heaven was not in place to enable the continuous flow of the river? How many of our cities and communities suffer because believers do not embrace the full government of Heaven?

The Bride is moving out of the place where she is about a person and a gifting. Every believer is gifted with the same Holy Spirit. It is the government of Heaven that enables the saints to be the splendid Bride. It's not that there are not leaders called into Heaven's government; it is that we are moving rapidly into a time when government comes before leader, a time when leaders embrace the government and serve it as God's plan to nurture and mature His glorious Bride.

Interestingly, Saul, the one God chose to be king, is cowering in fear, but David, who is anointed to be king but not yet in the office, advances to the fight. Both of the men have the apostolic call on their lives. God removed the call from Saul and gave it to David. Why? Saul disobeyed. But Saul did not just disobey God; he violated God's government by rejecting the prophet Samuel. The foundation of God's government is apostolic and prophetic. Victory cannot occur when the two will not walk together or when they are ignored altogether. The brook that contained the victory for God's kingdom was always present and always contained the five smooth stones.

It could just as easily have been Saul who saw the blueprint for victory, put aside the natural instruments of warfare, went to the brook, and took the stones to defeat Goliath. He couldn't do that because he did not see God's government. He led from Earth toward Heaven, rather than from Heaven to earth. God is enabling His body to receive the magnificent revelation of His government. He is enabling His Bride to come forth in this time on the planet to bring victory to nations, cities, towns, families, and people. She is bringing the fullness of Heaven to Earth like never before: *"But you are a chosen race, a royal priesthood, a holy nation, a people for God's own possession, so that you may proclaim the excellencies of Him who has called you out of darkness into His marvelous light."*⁷

The Glorious Bride is arising. She has come into a place of great momentum. She has re-covenanted with her Bridegroom. She has a greater revelation than ever before of God's plan for her to be spectacular on earth. She is more aware now than ever before of the price of the shed blood of Jesus her Bridegroom, paid to clothe her in amazing glory. She has matured to the point that she is no longer rejecting or ignoring the government of Heaven but understands she can never be all she was intended to be without Heaven's government.

She now refuses to be known as a Bride who accepts her Bridegroom but not His government. She is no longer saving her glory for some future moment, but she has decided with everything in her to live in the greatest, most splendid, and spectacular demonstration of Heaven here on Earth that has ever been witnessed. She now understands that being spectacular, glorious, a chosen generation, a royal priesthood, a holy nation, and a peculiar people is not for the exclusion of humanity but for the benefit of it. She now knows that the glory about to be displayed by the King's Bride here on Earth will bring solutions to the earth's greatest challenges, renew cites and nations, and provoke the whole Earth to jealousy when they see her grandeur.

She is about to shock the mountains of culture with creativity, love, ideas, entertainment, medical breakthroughs, and excellence in all she does. The culture will be so amazed it will come out of its darkness and into His marvelous light. The Bride is about to make history. I am privileged to be a part of this great move of God on the earth and am overwhelmed by what God has in store for the generations to come. Here Comes the Bride.

ENDNOTES

1. Revelation 19:7-9
2. Revelation 19:7
3. John 18:33-36
4. Acts 1:6-8
5. Acts 1:8
6. Isaiah 60:3
7. 1 Peter 2:9

MEET THE AUTHOR

David Brudnicki is a teacher, church leader, coach and visionary. He currently leads an inner-city house of worship which he assumed leadership of as a church re-plant in 2002. He invests his life into the vision of enabling people to reach their God-given destiny and purpose, and seeing the Bride of Christ arise in His city and beyond.

David has worked in corporate America for over thirty years in various management and leadership roles for a Fortune 500 company. His leadership style has evolved from a technically-focused approached to a people-focused approach as he developed a deep passion for the art and science of leadership. He holds a bachelor's degree in Information Technology and a Masters of Arts degree in Technology Management. He is currently pursuing a second Masters of Arts in Organizational Leadership.

David, and his amazing wife Ruth, have been married for over thirty years. They have raised three children who all possess a passion to see the Glorious Bride arise in their lifetime.

WANT TO WORK WITH DAVID?

David is available to speak and impart anointing for Heaven's government and for leadership at the individual and corporate level.

Some of David's Topics Are:

- Heaven's Government
- The Glorious Bride
- The Manifestation of the Sons and Daughters of God
- Leadership from the Five Functions of Heaven's Government (for the individual, married couples, and corporate bodies)
- Submission and Alignment to Proper Authority and Godly Servant-Leadership Authority

David also has extensive coaching experience with both individuals, pre-marital couples, and married couples. He also has a deep passion to see young believers develop their God given leadership skills for the next great awakening.

Contact David at:
David12b@verizon.net
www.Leadersserv1st.com

WORKS CITED

- *The Bible:* King James Version. Cambridge: Cambridge UP, 1769.

- *The Bible.* The Message. Colorado Springs, CO: NavPress, 2004.

- *The Bible.* New American Standard Bible. Chicago: Moody, 1972.

- *The Bible:* New International Version. London: Hodder & Stoughton, 1984.

- Cabrera, Natasha J., Jay Fagan, Vanessa Wight, and Cornelia Schadler. "Influence of Mother, Father, and Child Risk on Parenting and Children's Cognitive and Social Behaviors." *Child Development,* vol. 82, no. 6, 2011, https://www.ncbi.nlm.nih.gov/pubmed/22026516. Accessed 4 August 2017.

- Gray, James M. "Only a Sinner Saved by Grace." *Hymnary.org,* https://hymnary.org/text/naught_have_i_gotten_but_what_i_received. Accessed 4 August 2017.

- *All Bible verses are from the New American Standard Bible, unless otherwise noted.*

www.ingramcontent.com/pod-product-compliance
Lightning Source LLC
Chambersburg PA
CBHW071121090426
42736CB00012B/1977